# MY TIME

*Me & You Together Infused in a Moment of Endearment*

# MY TIME

*Me & You Together Infused in a Moment of Endearment*

Marie Jenkins

Copyright © 2021 Marie Jenkins. All rights reserved.

To tell this story from her perspective, the author has attempted to recreate events, locales, and conversations from her memory and the memories of family members. The thoughts and expressions in this book are not necessarily those of the publisher but represent the author.

No part of this publication may be reproduced, distributed, or transmitted in any form or by any means, including photocopying, recording, or other electronic or mechanical methods, without the prior written permission of the author and publisher, except in the case of brief quotations embodied in critical reviews and specific other noncommercial uses permitted by copyright law.

Unless otherwise noted, all scriptures referenced are from the King James Version of the Bible, public domain.

For permission requests, please write to the publisher, addressed *Attention: Permissions Coordinator* to the address listed below.

First Printing, 2021

Library of Congress Number: 2021915136

ISBN(Hardback): 978-1-951883-77-5

The Butterfly Typeface Publishing
PO Box 56193
Little Rock AR 72215

## A Tribute to My Children

One of the most rewarding joys of my life was parenting my three children (Ron, Michele, and Michael). My life is enriched with gratification and overwhelming delight, as I have watched their growth and maturity to adulthood. Each day reminds me how blessed I am for being given the privilege of being their "Mother."

I believe motherhood embodies the essence and characteristics of Jesus, Christ: love, compassion, forgiveness, patience; nurturer, protector. With full confidence, I entrust my legacy and our family's continued story to be remembered and repeated through their life journeys. Ron, Michele, and Michael, I love you always.

Mom

> "My child, never forget the things I have taught you. Trust in the Lord with all your heart; do not depend on your own understanding. Seek His will in all you do, and He will show you which path to take."
> (Proverb 3:1, 5-6 (NLT)

"Before your development in your mother's womb,
I started your story..." God.

**Jeremiah 29:11**

## Table of Contents

The Beginning ........................................................... 11
My Father ................................................................. 19
My Mother ............................................................... 25
Introduction: An Evolution of a Life ....................... 31
Chapter One: My Childhood ................................. 35
Chapter Two: Conquering the Monsters .............. 43
Chapter Three: Storytime ...................................... 49
Chapter Four: An Old Soul .................................... 53
Chapter Five: David ............................................... 59
Chapter Six: Master of The Pots ........................... 65
Chapter Seven: Michael ........................................ 71
Chapter Eight: Life ................................................. 75
Chapter Nine: Life .................................................. 85
Chapter Ten: Germany .......................................... 89
Chapter Eleven: Visions ........................................ 95
Chapter Twelve: Lost in Sorrow .......................... 103
Chapter Thirteen: Acclimating ............................. 111
Chapter Fourteen: Returning to the States ........ 117
Chapter Fifteen: An Ending ................................. 125
Chapter Seventeen: Enjoying Life ....................... 135
Chapter Eighteen: Through the Valley ............... 145
Chapter Nineteen: Flying Colors ......................... 151
Chapter Twenty: Songs of Zion .......................... 157
Chapter Twenty-One: Unforsaken ...................... 165
Chapter Twenty-Two: The Breath of God .......... 175

Chapter Twenty-Three: Miracle ................................................. 187
Chapter Twenty-Four: Shut Down .............................................. 195
Chapter Twenty-Five: Another Ending ........................................ 205
Chapter Twenty-Six: Thank You Jesus ....................................... 211
Chapter Twenty-Seven: Widowhood ........................................... 221
Chapter Twenty-Eight: Normalcy ................................................ 225
Chapter Twenty-Nine: The Wings of Christ ................................ 233
Chapter Thirty: A Good and Faithful Servant ............................. 237
Chapter Thirty-One: Love Is in The Air ...................................... 243
Chapter Thirty-Two: Your Blessing ............................................. 249
Chapter Thirty-Three: My Kind of Man ....................................... 253
Chapter Thirty-Four: Standing on His Word .............................. 259
Chapter Thirty-Five: A Garment of Praise .................................. 263
Conclusion: Finally, Marie ......................................................... 269
Photo Gallery ............................................................................. 276
Photo Gallery continued ............................................................ 282
About the Author ....................................................................... 287

# Foreword

Some will say I have saved *the best for last*. A statement that is well supported. I am currently *living my best life*. There is a new chapter in my life, which I have embraced with thanksgiving. Being thankful is a reminder of prior difficulties. I endured multiple seasons of struggle in my life. I am the survivor of the deaths of two husbands: Ron's father and then Michele and Michael's father. After the last death occurred, I had no desire for another Holy Matrimony. I was resigned to being content with widowhood.

During this time, my children were grown and pursuing their life careers. They encouraged me to find love again. However, I was not in a place where I was ready to commit or submit to another marriage. For the first time in my life, I was alone. I was an empty nester. I could feel the stillness of the house speaking to me in silence.

I buried my thoughts in prayer and in the Word of God. I was matriculating through Carlow University perusing the completion of a Bachelor of Arts Degree in Social Work, minor in Psychology and Theology. What I would wear the next day was most prevalent in my planning. The transition of my life had come full circle. Despite the fullness of a daily agenda, my heart was in despair. I experienced sadness which accompanied me in my struggle as I searched to find a place of solace and comfort. I welcomed times of reflections on a kaleidoscope of precious memories and events: birthday celebrations, holidays, family gatherings, graduations, new life and even the devastation of finality-death.

Often, I could hear laughter and children running through the house. There were times I thought I smelled a turkey basting in the oven or the Temptations singing "This Christmas," entertaining my family while we danced and trimmed the Christmas tree.

Our family guard dog (Buffy) died several years prior to me retiring from the Penn Hills School District. After six months of retirement, I reentered the work force at Mercy Behavior Health, Pittsburgh, Pennsylvania. I accepted the position as the Administrator to the Director of Service Coordination.

My duties and responsibilities did not end with the workday. I, along with my two brothers (Joe and Mike), were the caregivers to my parents. Each one of us took a shift providing twenty-four-hour *personal* care for our parents. My commitment to the church embodied not only my body but my soul. As a District Missionary (an honorable position bestowed by the Church of God In Christ denomination), I was responsible to provide spiritual leadership to the Women's Ministry, comprised of five area churches.

Still matriculating through Carlow University, we laid our father to rest. My mother's health soon took a steep decline which required twenty-four-hour *professional* assistance.

I was driven by the urgency of my responsibilities. My days were full. Yet, at times I felt so alone. After thirteen years, I reached a season of maturity (I will elaborate later.). God granted me tremendous favor when I said to Him, "Lord, if it is in your perfect will, I now desire a husband."

My sincere prayer is that as you read *My Story* you will be saturated with appreciation of the "now" blessings bestowed to me by God. One of which has become my "whole new world." I hope that *My Story* will compel those who are in life struggles to hold on to faith and trust God as He brings you through them into the abundance of life.

My entire life, from a toddler to senior status, is a testimony of how God's awesome power, grace, mercy, forgiveness, and healing sustained my life during this journey. For those who will commit to my writing, I desire that it will strengthen your faith in knowing that God is the giver and sustainer of life. He is the Alpha and Omega. We have our being in Him. All that we are and will ever be is because of His grace and mercy. Hope for today and eternal life rest in His son Jesus.

It is **M.Y. T.I.M.E.** (*Me & You Together Infused in a Moment of Endearment!*) to share **M.Y. S.T.O.R.Y.** (*My Year Starts Today On the Roads of Yesterday!*).

And I feel privileged and honor to share the journey with you. May these words provide you with encouragement and the reliance of The Lord. Now, on to *My Story*.

Marie Jenkins

Dear Reader,

It is a great honor and pleasure to pen just a few comments in Marie's autobiography. The "buttons are popping off my shirt with pride" to witness yet another of her many accomplishments. However, this one will not be just shared locally, but with the world!

Yes, Marie is my wife, lover, very best friend, and confidant whom God has designed for me. As you read about her life, you will discover the grit, power, and humor she applies to life's challenges, sorrows, and obstacles that I have come to know.

All her many gifts and talents are held together with a heart of love, compassion, and fierce family protection. The unwritten gifts of Marie that are only known by family and friends (i.e., her God-given anointing, unwavering love for God, a self-taught musician, singer, wonderful homemaker, and fantastic cook) are by no means an all-encompassing list. However, many will be revealed as you walk with her through the pages of this book.

Marie, I love you with all my heart and am so very proud of what God has enabled you to sustain and accomplish.

Maurice Jenkins (AKA Babe)

*"I believe that I can do all things through Christ who strengthens me!"*
**Philippians 4:13**

## Acknowledgment(s)

This book is made possible by the leading of the Holy Spirit, God's grace, the encouragement of my husband (Maurice), and my children (Ron, Michele, and Michael).

## Honorable Mentions

People who have been and continue to provide significant support, encouragement, empowerment, prayers and love:

Mother Verna Shields, Mother Martha Stevenson, Eugene & Sandra Petty,

Casandra McAdams, Michael & Linda Anderson, LaTonya Clark, Elder Rikki Edwards,

Mary Priester, Diane Taylor-Johnson, John & Karen Parker, Jacquelyn McDonald,

Miyoshi Gordon Ph.D.,

Wilma Beauford, Ph.D., Clinton Beauford, Pastor; Byron Stevenson, Pastor

Bernadette Fletcher Ph.D., Nancy Hines Ph.D., Theron Wade Ph.D.,

Norma Woodard Ph.D., Reverend Frank Woodard, Willie C Barnes, Pastor

Bishop Kevin McCree Ph.D., Evette McCee, Joyce Davis

Iris M. Williams, Author & Publisher

# M.Y. T.I.M.E.

Before starting my workday, I had morning prayer. Still in the moment of thanksgiving, the Lord gave me the phrase, "my time." Nothing else was revealed. Several days passed and I was still weighing in my mind the meaning of the phrase. With the same urgency, the Lord later revealed to me that the phrase was an acronym, representing our time spent together:

*Me & You: Together Infused in a Moment of Endearment*

This revelation compelled me to write my story.

# M.Y. S.T.O.R.Y.

While working on the book, I had a similar, profound encounter with the Lord. A second phrase was given to me, "my story."

This time I was given revelation, including the acronym:

*My Years, Start Today on the Roads of Yesterday*

Being redirected with clarity, gave me a more concise narrative with a broader appeal. This is the first time in my life where my thoughts are free flowing and unhindered by its contents. I can remember childhood experiences as if they were present day events. I have pondered different situations (some pleasant, some not so pleasant), yet my emotions are not held captive by their negative outcomes. I am present in the moment. When I measure my current being, verses yesterday's actions, I reflect on the evolution of my emotions. I have shed the weight of sadness, the burden of depression, as well as the responsibility of unacceptance.

This opportunity to share my life journey will show the abundance of blessings received throughout my life.

My pilgrimage has enlarged my tent providing several opportunities to pursue my passions. I have tried to correct unfavorable choices that derailed forward movement.

Longevity has allowed me to a be recipient of rewarding venues, to experience growth and maturity and to witness the adulthood of my three grown children. My estate has been enlarged by treasures of God's promises extended to me through my grandchildren, great-grandchildren, a daughter-n-love and a son-n-love.

I am humbled to share my testimony with family, friends, and an audience who will appreciate struggle, hope, and victory.

The pages that follow will unfold the character of my story, statue of my struggles, purpose of my pain and unveil my passions. I am blessed to contribute my words in print.

This book will chronicle the height and depth of my testimony.

I pray that my story will encourage you to never give up or give in to the pressures of life.

Don't lose hope in the fight. Hold on to your integrity, reenergize your mind with knowledge, and seek God's purpose for your life.

Allow daily devotions to keep your peace stable.

May you be granted God's best,

*Marie Jenkins*

# The Foundation

*Marie Jenkins', My Time*

# The Beginning

*A Stacked Deck*

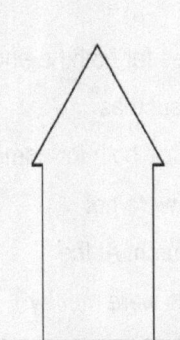

*At the time, my dad was only six years old and the youngest of his parents' children. His sister Mable was eight, and his brother Johnny was ten. Dad told us that the family salvaged as much as they could for their journey to the north.*

*"I remember some of our neighbors stopping by with tears, kisses, and well wishes for safety and God's speed," Dad recalled. "I never saw my father again, and I never knew what happened to him."*

My father was a proud Pentecostal Pastor, ordained and licensed by the Church of God in Christ. Dad dedicated more than fifty years to the Ecclesiastical call. His Pastoral responsibilities embodied his entire being. His passion for preaching the Word of God honed his development and unfurled him into a man of great faith and integrity. Being filled with God's love molded his meekness, augmented his patience, expanded his tolerance to temperance, and elongated his capacity for suffering. Whether he was teaching, preaching, or studying God's Word, it displayed his love for Christ. The Lord truly was the joy of his life.

The call to Pastor a church congregation also came with a mandate and responsibility of raising a young family, one daughter (me) and five sons. In addition to pastoring a church and raising a family, he worked full time for the Department of Revenue, United States Government.

The deck was stacked.

There were numerous physical and financial challenges for both he and my mother. Sometimes hard decisions were required such as addressing the competing requirements of utility bills due both for home and church. Often the income from tithes and offering were not substantial enough to cover utility expenses for the church. At the beginning of his ministry, any church financial shortfalls were met by personal sacrifices and declining church compensation. Even when the church experienced congregational growth and could adequately cover the financial obligations required, my father remained reluctant to accept any Pastoral offerings.

When I got older, I would remind my dad of **1 Timothy 5:18b KJV**, "...*the laborer is worthy of his reward.*"

Needless to say, my advice was ignored for many years.

Dad's dedication not only left him financially depleted, but each morning, despite mental tiredness and physical exhaustion, he went to work.

In addition to mental and physical stress, my father was also impacted by an injury sustained in his youth. Early in his young life, my father had worked in a coal mine to provide financial support for grandmother and two siblings. His lower right leg suffered a severe laceration that only worsened due to a lack of medical attention. The injury caused painful bleeding ulcers which almost claimed his life, twice.

The long tradition of family Thanksgiving dinner had always been held at my parents' house. We always looked forward to the gathering. However, over the years, we noticed subtle things about our parents. At first it was minor things like the greying of their hair. The tint of gray around the temples of my father became the hallmark of his distinguished look and character. Mom's waves and curls glistened in the brightness and were worn like a crown. Her hair reflected a seasoned woman of grace and elegance and revealed the story of a virtuous woman, called blessed. Although Mom wore longevity graciously, that did not stop her from jokingly blaming my father for any gray she may have had.

In addition to the cosmetic changes my parents experienced, we also noticed that they did not walk as fast and were not as agile. Senility set in with Dad and Mom's mobility became limited to a wheelchair. The reality soon became that my parents were older and no longer able to carry out the preparation or cooking required for such a large Thanksgiving gathering as we had all become accustomed. So, I invited the family to share Thanksgiving dinner with my family. Thus began the new tradition of family gatherings.

One year in particular stands out in my memory.

After dinner, the family was still seated around the dining room table, anticipating my famous sweet potato pie topped with extra creamy whip cream. I began to slice the pie, serving it from my right side, to be passed along to the next person. A slice had not reached my dad when he began to share with us the story of his childhood.

"When I was a child," he began with a voice that demanded attention, "my dad was forced to leave our home and family business in Bessemer, Alabama." His calmness quieted us.

My father's family business was a General Store where fruits, vegetables, and dry goods could be purchased. The store extended credit to families who were experiencing hard times.

Apparently, my grandfather had returned to the store from an errand of some kind.

"When **my father returned** and entered the front of the store, he heard noises coming from the back storage area. He walked around the front counter to the storage room and witnessed an intimate encounter between his wife and a man named Billy."

The family sat eagerly anticipating the story.

My father described how his father, "...in a fit of rage and strength, took the man's life with his bare hands."

Shocked, we slowly exhaled.

Dad picked up his fork and took his first bite of sweet potato pie. He readjusted his body in the chair, took a deep breath and collected his thoughts. I could tell he was experiencing discomfort at remembering what must have been a painful memory. There was sadness in his voice when he continued. We waited patiently.

Finally, he said, "Days went by, and no one from the family saw my father, again. People from the town began asking about the man my daddy killed. A search party came into the store asking Granny and my mother when was the last time they saw that fellow. Then they asked where my daddy was."

"Most of the people in town were friendly enough towards the family," my father said as he chewed on his pie. "Granny was a mid-wife and would be called upon to deliver their children. The towns people made purchases from our General Store. They knew us as good folks."

After Dad finished his pie, he wiped his mouth and pushed his chair back from the table. Thankfully, he continued the story. "The wife of the preacher warned my family that our lives were in danger. She said a mob of white men were planning to hang all of us, starting with me and my brother! She said that there was a witness who saw Billy enter the back door of our store."

Visibly shaken and wrestling with his emotions, Dad forced himself to finish what he started. "My mother and grandmother packed as much of our family's belongings that would fit into our wagon." His eyes became glassy as he endured the pain of telling us how they escaped. "That night all of us crawled into the wagon with my mother and grandmother in the driver's seat. My brother Johnny and sister Mable were safely covered in the rear of the wagon."

At the time, my dad was only six years old and the youngest of his parents' children. His sister Mable was eight, and his brother Johnny was ten. Dad told us that the family salvaged as much as they could for their journey to the north.

"I remember some of our neighbors stopping by with tears, kisses, and well wishes for safety and God's speed," Dad recalled. "I never saw my father again, and I never knew what happened to him."

My father's family settled in West Virginia.

"I am sure my mother was riddled with pain and guilt over her actions that caused our family to become separated and uprooted," Daddy speculated.

Despite how she may have felt, my grandmother and her children made their home in Cherry Valley, Burgettstown, Pennsylvania. Granny had a parcel of land where she had a small brick house. The rooms were small, three to be exact: living room, bedroom, and kitchen. In the rear of the house stood a narrow, tall wooden box, called the outhouse. Adjacent was a well, where fresh spring water was drawn.

Opening the front door ushered one's presence into the living room. In the middle of the floor stood a black potbelly stove that looked like a roaring inferno when one opened its door. In the front of the stove was a heavy rod iron door with peek-a-boo holes and a rod iron handle that was hot to the touch. The pot belly's warmth was activated when fed wooden logs and was the only heating source for the tiny home.

With only one bedroom, granny and my aunt Mable shared a bed. The house was not insulated. When the wind blew, one could gauge the direction it was coming from: north, south, east or west. On the other side of the room, my dad and my uncle Johnny shared a twin bed.

When granny was summoned to deliver a baby, she would sometimes leave my dad and his siblings for weeks.

"We were not allowed to go outside," my father told us, "except to go to the outhouse or to clean the chicken coop."

It was during this time that he developed a love for the Lord. While feeding the chickens, he would deliver a message of hope to them he told us.

At the age of thirteen, my father decided he wanted to go see his mother. With permission from granny, he walked close to five miles before reaching the address given to him.

"When I arrived," my father said slowly, "she was not happy to see me. She was living with a man."

*Marie Jenkins', My Time*

The conversation between he and his mother was shallow and hurried. As a young boy he was sad and overcome with feelings of rejection. He had not seen his mother since they left the South. My father overheard the man say to his mother, "I ain't taking care of no kids. Send him back where he came from."

My dad was so hurt. She did not even defend her own son. Feeling unwanted and unwelcomed, he turned towards the door to leave.

"Wait," he heard her cry.

Daddy thought that maybe the man had changed his mind. He turned around in anticipation only to see her standing there with a sack. Instead of offering him a home, all she had for him was a peanut butter sandwich, apple, and jar of freshly made lemon-aid.

"Go home," she said and kissed him on the cheek.

# My Father

*Grace and Legacy*

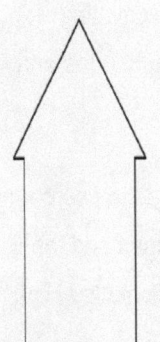

*My father's days were stressful. Many times, after working eight-hour days for the government he returned home to work on a broken furnace or stop a constantly dripping bathroom faucet. The stress and continuous movement placed pressure on his legs, which would cause his ankles to swell and the laceration on his leg to open and contributed to blood clots forming. Consequently, there were several near-death experiences due to an infection in his leg. There were numerous emergency trips by ambulance to the hospital for blood clots threatened his heart.*

My father returned home to find his Granny frail and sickly.

Her health was quickly deteriorating. She was no longer able to work. Sickness had stricken her fragile body. His sister, Mable was given extra household responsibilities, which she rebelled against. His eldest brother, Johnny left home. The chickens my father once preached too were long gone. They had become Sunday dinners. The cupboards no longer housed Granny's canned fruits or jelly-jams.

At the age of fourteen, with only an eight-grade education, my dad began working in a restaurant/bar earning five dollars a week to help support his family. He also worked on a farm for one dollar a day. To compensate for his pay, he was given potatoes, onions, bread, chickens, and greens. Later he worked as a coal miner.

Striving to keep food on the table, my father also worked as a sandhog. A sandhog was a term used for a worker involved in excavating underneath the Monongahela River. It entailed building bridges and tunnel foundations.

Daddy served in the United States Army and became a staff sergeant. After his discharge, he resumed working in the coal mines and the building trades while attending night school to earn a Schenley High School diploma.

In 1956, my father was employed by the Internal Revenue Service. To improve his work for the government, Dad studied accounting for two years at the University of Pittsburgh with completion. With hard work, dedication and determination, my father started a refrigeration business, purchased his first Model T Ford, and had his suits tailor-made.

Granny loved my father and taught him the love of Christ, which took root and compelled him in 1959 to answer the call as an ordained Elder by the late Bishop Gordon E. Vaughn prelate of the First Ecclesiastical Jurisdiction Churches of God in Christ, Western Pennsylvania. In 1961, my father was installed as Pastor of Religious Center C.O.G.I.C. (3412

Ligionier Street) in Pittsburgh, Pennsylvania. He remolded the church (which was a shell on the inside) and burned the mortgage in four and a half years with a membership of about twenty parishioners and family members.

As a pastor, Dad devoted himself to underprivileged, destitute, disabled adults and narcotic addicts. My father's devotion to people less fortunate earned him praise, respect and admiration within the Pittsburgh Community and Tri-State area. He was truly a dedicated servant of God. Throughout his tenure, my father was the beneficiary of numerous accolades. His compassion helped to improve so many lives.

He was recognized by his supervisor and peers for his work ethics and sympathetic consciousness of others.

October 12, 1972, on behalf of the Chief Intelligence Division of the Internal Revenue Service, a letter of commendation was sent on behalf of my father. In a memorandum addressed to the Office of President Richard Nixon, a request was granted that Revenue Agent Samuel Williams be awarded a Humanitarian plaque.

After twenty-seven years with the Internal Revenue Service, Dad retired to full time ministry.

As a young boy, my father endured tragedies, hardships, disappoints and rejections. Dad never lost his focus or joy. Every morning he sang songs of Zion, thanking God for another day. One of his favorite tunes,

"Just another day that the Lord has kept me," was followed by a loud banging on our bedroom doors and him saying, "It is time to get up!"

My father's days were stressful. Many times, after working eight-hour days for the government he returned home to work on a broken furnace or stop a constantly dripping bathroom faucet. The stress and continuous movement placed pressure on his legs, which would cause his ankles to swell and the laceration on his leg to open and contributed to blood clots forming. Consequently, there were several near-death experiences due to an infection in his leg. There were numerous emergency trips by ambulance to the hospital for blood clots threatened his heart.

Despite difficult challenges and struggles, he endured! I never heard him complain.

But I did hear him often praying to the Lord for mercy. He never gave up on his covenant commitment to God nor the commitment as a father and husband. The disappointments he faced, or setbacks experienced only made him more determined to finish the race he started a long time ago. My father persevered through some of life's most significant challenges and won! My dad is my hero! Even when he had aged, and his movements were restricted, he continued to quote scriptures and could tell you where they were found in the Bible. One of his favorite scripture was **2 Timothy 4:7,** which states, *"I have fought a good fight. I have finished my course. I have kept the faith."*

Before God called him home to rest, I was able to tell Dad how much I loved and respected him. I let him know that the greatest gift he gave me was the introduction to Jesus Christ. Often, I will whisper, "I am still holding on."

I bestow the greatest honor with the appropriate terminology of "hero" upon my father. He was endowed with a relentless strength. His achievements and ability to complete tasks gave credence to his untiring belief in God. He is found as a "man" of Godly character and principles. My father is not measured by the standard of legendary fictional figures or literary tales. He was a central figure who impacted not only my life but all those he encountered. He had a strong constitution of beliefs that navigated his moral compass.

God blessed my father's life with His grace. I am sure that I am not only a recipient of my Heavenly father's grace, but I am also living in my earthly father's legacy.

Photo 1  Author's parents:

*Reverend Samuel Williams: Dad, Pastor, Mentor and Maude Williams: Mother, Best Friend, Proctor in childhood, (I was her Advocate in her senior years)*

# My Mother

*A Fragrant Garment of Honor*

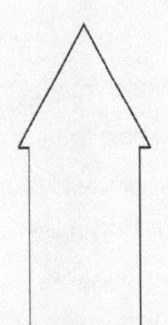

> *I think of her daily and miss our phone calls and the stories she would share with me. Often her stories were repeated over and over, but I stilled enjoyed them as much as the first time I heard them. My mother was a great storyteller. She not only spoke with dramatization, but she also had body gyrations to emphasize her points. Inside of her vault were chronicles of events she shared that shaped her personality. She was the sum total of "distinction."*

**M**any of my father's accomplishments were shared with me throughout the years by my precious mother.

Her prayers, devotion, love, and painstaking sacrifices undergirded my father and his endeavors as one. Mother was five feet one inch, yet, she stood tall beside my father, who was six feet one inch, for fifty-two years of marriage. She actively worked in the church with him for over forty-five years, teaching Sunday school, coordinating various church events, raising four children, all while pursuing her career as a licensed Registered Nurse. My mother found a way to make it all work with the resources that were made available to her.

The church was not financially solvent due to low membership and the need for renovations. When my father purchased the church, it had been vacant for quit sometime. Extensive renovations were intimate. The roof was leaking. The sanctuary was a hollow shell. My mother agreed with my father's plea to use our home as collateral to obtain a mortgage for the church and extra funds for the project of needed renovations.

The financial struggles that my parents had kept my mother from acquiring the desires of her heart, in order to keep the home lights burning due to the encumbered weighted debt. My mother would take extra hospital shifts from time to time for additional pay. The added income blessed our home and liquidated some financial obligations.

The night shift was favorable to Mother not only to compensate the family finances, but to avoid the need to hire sitters. The decision to continue this practice took a toll on her body, as well as her heart over being separated from the family. But at the time when the need of having a two-income household confronted my parents, the decision was agreed upon to move forward with the plan.

There were mornings when she had to use public transpiration to return home. In winter months she suffered from the cold weather. My dad had to leave for work before she arrived. My God mother (who lived with us) would watch us until my mother got home. Caring for two sick children (brother David, sickle cell and myself, extreme eczema) presented her greatest demands. She, too, struggled beyond her own pain to financially contribute to the family.

My mother was also challenged with tremendous obstacles. Medically she was diagnosed as an anemic. She was always cold and tired. In later years, her condition placed a strain on her health. Years of working the graveyard shift (11:00 p.m. to 7:00 a.m.) flustered her with guilt knowing that her four children were on the mercy of their father. *Dad slept without being disturbed by the crying whimpers or frightened boogie-man sightings.*

My brothers and I suffered the most not having access to her in times of need. My mother lived with the guilt of her decisions. Later, I found out how she lived with it. Before she transitioned from this earth to glory, she shared much of her thoughts, experiences, regrets and her heart strings with me. They were difficult to hear, and I struggled to control my tears. Visibly, my emotions were stoic. But tears were streaming down the inter most part of my being into my heart. I was overwhelmed with grief as I treaded the path of her pain. At that moment, I realized the unselfish decisions she had made on behalf of the love she had for her family.

My mother never received an Oscar, nor a Tony or a Grammy. Neither was her name on the lips of those who called others for their achievements. But she was the "Best" that God created for us and others as well. I pray that I can embody her fragrance and wear her garment of honor.

I think of her daily and miss our phone calls and the stories she would share with me. Often her stories were repeated over and over, but I stilled enjoyed them as much as the first time I heard them. My mother was a great storyteller. She not only spoke with dramatization, but she also had body gyrations to emphasize her points. Inside of her vault were chronicles of events she shared that shaped her personality. She was the sum total of "distinction."

I am confident she is living her best life now.

My mom was ready to join my father in the presence of Jesus.

She has passed from death to life eternal. Finally, she can now enjoy the fruit of her earthly labor: Pain free, no debt, no sorrow, no worries, and a crown of jewels for a life well lived.

*"Many daughters have done virtuously; but thou excellest them all."*
**Proverbs 31:29**

Yes, my mother was the optimum of the Proverb 31 woman.

*"Her children arise up, and call her blessed; her husband also, and he praiseth her."*
**Proverb 31:28**

I welcome her legacy as well which is steeped within my being.

My parents' struggles were insurmountable. Despite the seemingly harsh realities of life they endured, they both demonstrated through their walk of faith what it means to be a "good soldier" for Christ. Through the complexities of anguish, misplaced pain, and shadows of darkness, I realize they made it only by God's grace, His mercy, and their commitment to Him.

Even now, as I reflect on those formative years of my life, I realize how much I gleaned from their examples. I still glean today. They left me with a pictorial tapestry filled with legacy, truth, and good works.

I believe, someday when I have passed on from this life, there will be a reunion with my parents in Heaven.

What a celebration it will be!

Until we meet again, enjoy your rest.

*Photo 2 Author's parents: Until death do we part...50 Years of marriage!*

# Introduction: An Evolution of a Life

*A Foundation of Family, Community, and Faith*

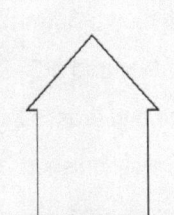

*I Thank God for His promise that allows me to enjoy the fruits of my labor! I have reached a serenity of time and space that refreshes me. The setlines of a new day dawning remind me of what the Bible declares new mercy given each morning.*

We lived in a neighborhood of diversity until the 1960 riots. Prior to the riots, our neighbors were made up of Italians, Jews, Afro-Americans, as well as Caucasian families. Social distancing was not encouraged! We all played together, shared food, street games, walked to school and fought against other neighborhood kids who invaded our territory. If some stores did not want to serve the Afro-American community, no one would patronize that business.

Collectively, community celebrations included Santa Claus riding inside a fire truck, passing out candy to all the children. Fire fighters released water from fire hydrants as a jester of good will and wholesome fun.

Many of my friend's parents managed small business. Therefore, our dollars spent stayed within the economic borders of our town and sustained our neighborhoods. Our parents did not have to leave the community for groceries, clothing, or banking.

The P.T.A. (Parent Teacher Association) Elementary school meetings were diverse family gatherings with the principle and teachers ending with refreshments in the gym. The Arts department provided entertainment for parents and featured something from their child(ren): choir, band, science projects with moving parts, and/or featured art exhibits. Everyone that night was on their best behavior and dressed appropriately for the evening. Fathers were always the distinguished guest since they hardly ever came. Their presence commanded excellence, growth, achievements, and most of all, approval. Grades were discussed, areas of "need improvement" were recognized with State Standard educational plans of accomplishment offered by teachers.

The love for Jesus Christ was instilled in me at an early age by my parents. They supported my adolescent vow to salvation. As my love for Christ grew, so did the love for His people and the ministerial work of the church. The church was and still is my solace, sanctuary, and my place of creativity. The atmosphere of His glory engulfs my inter-person with enhanced joy and revelation of His Word.

My parents never gave up on my joy of praise, my hunger for the Word of God, or the music inside my heart. So many of the older Saints that I grew up with have transitioned from this life. They too sowed much of their time toward me and my journey to Christian maturity. They joined my parents in partnership with their support as I began to blossom in the foundation of Holiness.

At this present time of my life, I am living in the moment referred to as *The Golden Years*. The front of my hair shows a stunning classical representation of maturity through the lens of shining silver. The glistening of the sun illuminates the richness of my senior status. I have learned to take it *slow*. I do not have a need to dart in and out of traffic or break speeding laws to get home before the children. Nor do I need to pick up the pace when doing laundry, preparing meals, or cleaning house. I can take my time and march to the beat of my own rhythm. The weekends are mine to roam the mall, take in a movie, have lunch on the strip or just sit and watch the beauty of each day. I do not set alarm clocks and I do not have a curfew for bedtime. I am retired!

Thank God for His promise that allows me to enjoy the fruits of my labor! I have reached a serenity of time and space that refreshes me. The setlines of a new day dawning remind me of what the Bible declares new mercy given each morning.

Fresh brewed coffee, sitting at the breakfast nook table, evokes a conversation at length with the Lord. Time is lost in prayer and in His presence. I patiently wait for His response. I give time to remember memories, some pleasant, some unpleasant. Together they have become the bedrock of my personality, my achievements, my failures, and thank Heavens my second chances. These adorning years permit me the opportunity to be at a present state, allowing my thoughts take me back to the roads of yesterday. My most compelling story is being told thru the lens of my life experiences. They unveil a life shaped by trials, tribulations, setbacks, heroic events, and God moments.

I am blessed to share this journey through direct participation of knowledge and wisdom that I have obtained through various venues. I am confident the words you read on the following pages will not just entertain your curiosity but also appeal to the story inside you. My sincere prayer for you, the reader of *My Story*, is that it will inspire and bless you to never give up in your faith and to make a difference.

# Chapter One: My Childhood

*Stolen Joy*

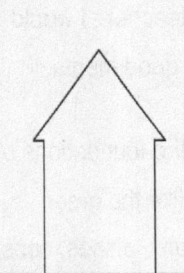

> *When I turned two years old, I developed an itchy skin rash marked by the medical term: Eczema. This eruption in my body stole the joy of my playful imaginations. It caused my young life to be alienated from the delight of playing with other children. No one wanted to play with the little girl with scabs, boils, and running puss.*

I remember so vividly, most of my childhood. Three other persons (my aunt, my God mother DeeDee, and a member of the church) resided in the same house with our family. There were always adult conversations swirling. Some oral exchanges were humorous, some beyond my comprehension, and some disclosed dark family secrets. And you could be sure that following Sunday's church service there would be Monday morning dialogue that would last late into the night!

Our family joined in with the other church families for the *covered dish brigade* and the *breaking of bread*. My ears grew in size as I listened and retained the stories. Thunderous laughter echoed the hollow spaces of the house when one of the adult persons described the praise antics of one of the *sisters*.

"The Holy Spirit moved on sister so-and-so and revealed all her naked sins." This was followed by emulated body gyrations.

Each day, I would perch my small frame on the steps located between the first and second floor to ingest the tabloid-like stories. I never revealed any of the contents of the overheard conversations to anyone except my doll babies. I was their mother and schoolteacher. I would scold them of wrong doings and reward them for their good merits.

My childhood playtime, with my doll babies, reflected the foundations of my rearing. I had replicas of my mother's appliances like the green stove and refrigerator. I proudly displayed my pots, pans, dishes, cups, silverware, and napkins in the same fashion as my mother. One Christmas, I was told Santa left a ringer washer and dryer for my doll babies' clothes! I had everything I needed: crib for the babies, highchair for breakfast, groceries for the pantry, and a beauty parlor to do their hair. When winter turned into spring, I would take my doll babies for a stroll in the new buggy, around the neighborhood. I was a mother hen, watching over my prized possessions.

My obsession (and my possessions) with my doll babies was born of necessity.

When I turned two years old, I developed an itchy skin rash marked by the medical term: Eczema. This eruption in my body stole the joy of my playful imaginations. It caused my young life to be alienated from the joy of playing with other children. No one wanted to play with the little girl with scabs, boils and running puss. As I got older, I experienced segregation before it was brought to the forefront of society. I was teased, bullied, and ostracized. I was called horrible names that made me crawl inside of myself for comfort.

Every week my mother would take me to the free clinic for treatments. I had a young, white female Doctor by the name of Dr. Farney. She always greeted me with a smile. Yet I felt as if she was like all the rest, just amusing me and hoping not to have any physical contact with my skin.

Each clinic visit was worse than my last to my remembrance. My clothes would stick to the puss that ran from the creases of my arms, the back creases of my legs and the circumference of my neck. Although my entire body was peppered with sores, the worse drainage was from my body creases. I would cry as I was being disrobed for treatments. They would have to peel my clothing from the infected areas. Sometimes they would apply warm compresses to the outer layers of my clothing in hopes that it would soften the removal. The doctor would examine my condition to see if there were any improvements. I recognized my hopeless physical existence through her disappointing eyes and shallow voice. I watched the sadness in the eyes of my mother when Dr. Farney gave the prognosis of my condition, prescribing stronger cortisone cream, and pills with a steroid compound for the itching.

Being fully unrobed, I was instructed to step into a space just large enough to stand with my arms to my sides. I was not fully developed into womanhood, yet I felt invaded, embarrassed, ashamed, and wished that I were invisible. I would always ask God, "Why me?"

So that the ultraviolet light would not affect my eyes, I was given goggles. As I watched the doctor turn on the ultraviolet light, tears would flow from my eyes like a stream causing me to wish I had never been born. The light burst the puss oozed yellow fluid that filled pustules located in my head all the way down to the soles of my feet. I felt like a freak!

*Why couldn't this have happened to my brother instead of me?*

No one had an answer.

The procedure was designed to dry out the pustules and give me comfort. But instead, it dried my skin even more. The side effects were tortuous. My skin became thick, scaley, and drier. The outer layer of my skin resembled the appearance of a reptile.

Nights were the worse!

Night after night, before bed I was condemned to a sitz bath using an oatmeal substance intended to calm and moisturize my skin. Afterwards, my God mother would gently apply the prescribed cortisone cream. My parents would put white gloves on my hands to prevent me from scratching in my sleep. To be sure I didn't remove them, they would tie the top of the gloves around my small wrist with ribbon. Still, I would wake in the morning to a bed of new drainage, puss, and blood. Somewhere in the night I struggled to free my hands.

After the ultraviolet treatment with Dr. Farney, she would give me cortisone shots in my arm to help control the itch. Hours after the shots were administered my arm felt like it was carrying a piece of lead as a reminder of the experience. Not only was I sore and itchy, but I also felt like I was a burden and a curse to my family. None of my brothers were infected by this horrible, disfiguring disease. I believed that I was contaminated, an outcast.

I continued to question God.

*Why God? Don't you love me as much as you love my brothers? Did I do something bad to deserve this?*

Most of my days were sad I had only my doll babies to comfort me. They at least still wanted to play with me.

I welcomed rainy days. In my thoughts, I knew all the children were like me, they had to stay inside and play make-believe. Regardless of my limited mobility, I found various activities to occupy time. Other than my doll babies, the television was my closest companion.

I could always depend on favorite shows to entertain me. I was also amused by the role play my oldest brother would engage in from time to time. When he played Batman, he would get one of our mother's towels, place it around his neck, using a safety pin to fashion a cape, and off the steps he would jump, sailing through the air to apprehend suspects. From his lips he verbalized the same sounds from the television programming: Wham! Bam! Pow! Wow! I was amused by these actions. Other days, he would be Rifle Man or the Cowboy toting his rifle and wearing a gun belt below his hips. What a funny sight!

The only time I was invited into his adventures is when he needed a prisoner or a parishioner. As a prisoner, I would be hand cuffed and instructed to go to jail, which was the banister on the steps. I would spend a lot of time peeking through the spokes of the stairs waiting until someone bailed me out. As a parishioner, I played the piano, sang hymns, and passed around a plastic plate for the offering.

My brother preached the same message: "You need to come to church and be saved." After the benediction, he, I, and the congregation (my doll babies) would line-up on the steps, which miraculously transformed into the church van and my brother would safely drive us all home.

When we heard the voice of my mother calling out to us from the kitchen, "Kids! Get clean up that mess you've made, wash up and get ready for dinner." We knew our father would be home soon.

Just when I thought the day was rewarding with sibling play and maybe there would be promise for tomorrow, my brother would disturb the tranquility of my doll babies. He knocked my treasured doll babies over and said mean things to them!

Just like that, he became *The Joker* instead of *Batman*. Instead, of a hero, he was now a villain. I could not control my emotions. Tears swelled and flowed from my eye ducts. Screams emerged from my belly as I angrily swung in defense of my doll babies.

The actions of my brothers caused my body to perspire and itch incessantly. I yielded fully to the pressures of the moment. The more tense I became, the more worked up I became. Enticed by my brother's deviant antics, I became bloody from the scratching. Boils that had previously formed scabs, were now running with puss.

I quickly learned that stress was an enemy of my skin. For years I would struggle to not allow my environment to impact my emotions. If only I could just get some relief.

My whole being was aching from the incident.

Saddened by the outcome, I accepted his offering to help as I returned my doll babies to my bedroom.

*Marie Jenkins', My Time*

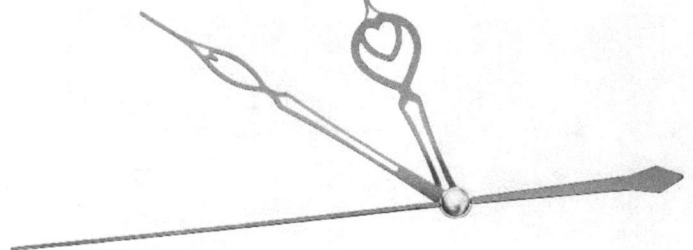

## Chapter Two: Conquering the Monsters

*Feeling Needed and Special*

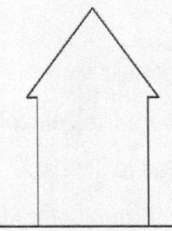

*These are some of my best memories, being needed by Mom and DeeDee.*

*They made me feel so special. Often, they would call my name to move the basket or check to see if the laundry outside was dry. They ran my little seventy-pound body until I was ready for an eight o'clock bedtime.*

I was born domesticated! I cleaned my bedroom without my parents asking me. I volunteered to wash the dishes, dust the furniture, run the sweeper on the carpet in the living room, and sweep and mop the kitchen floor. I especially looked forward to Mondays, which was the day my mother, God mother DeeDee and myself did the laundry.

The machine was taller than I, which meant that I always had to use a stepstool to participate. This prompted my father to build me a wooden box to stand on. The bottom of the washing machine set on four claw feet. The sight of them always made me quiver. Attached to the claw feet were four short white legs. The barrel of the washer was round and deep, with an agitator that looked like the propellers of a plane. I was fascinated by the appliance that keep my interest and desired to repeat the ritual every week.

*Marie Jenkins', My Time*

The wash machine was located in the basement of our home. We had to travel down a long, painful pair of steps that took you down into the coolness of the bottom of the house where it was *different*. One's nostrils had to conform to the aura of the room. It smelled like outside musk and if it had rained the day before, you could feel the dampness upon your skin.

Before we started, my mother would open the cellar door allowing additional light and fresh air to enter the room. There were five cement steps to climb once the door was opened that would lead to the back yard. With a bit of a struggle, Mom would pull the security iron bar that was stretched across two iron doors, giving clearance and allowing her to push open the doors. Once the doors were open, access was given to the back yard.

I was always eager to assist. The process to getting started was initiated when my mother turned the rusty faucet handle of the hot water into the basket of the washer. Once the tub was about a fourth filled, my mother would add the laundry detergent and Clorox. Two scoops of detergent and a half cup of Clorox. Yes, the first load of clothes were always the whites. (Prior to my post at the washing machine, I was responsible for separating the clothes by color. It made it easier for me and DeeDee to fill the tub on demand.)

I was instructed to place the white clothes in after the Clorox had be poured and allowed to swish around for a time. DeeDee always let me fill the basket. I took great pride in my assignments. Once the white clothes were all in, I would mimic the rotation of the washer's agitator going round and round with my head and eyes as I sang, "The wheels on the bus go round and round." Often DeeDee and Mom would join in on the chorus of the song.

After the completion of the first wash, the basket stood still, allowing the second and third process to occur.

It was time to rinse the clothes, but first they had to be fed into the wringer. DeeDee and I pulled each garment out of the hot soapy water and fed them one by one through the wringer. The wringer had two black rollers that squeezed the water from the garments. The wringer apparatus set above the washer and the rinse tub that was located on the opposite side of the washer. My mother manually turned the handle of the wringer located on the left. (She too, needed a step stool.) DeeDee and I fed the washed clothes, one by one, through the wringer. As they passed through, they would flatten out and drop into an aluminum bucket filled with rinse water. After the first rinse was accomplished, another aluminum bucket with clean water replaced the first. The same garments were re-entered into the wringer for the second rinse.

Once the bucket was filled, DeeDee and I would lift the handles and climb the concrete steps to the back yard. There were six rows of clothes lines supported by poles stretched across the entire back yard. My mother would bring a small wooden fruit basket with wooden clothes pins to hang the white clothes. (My father had lowered the clothes lines for our convenience.)

I took pride when DeeDee and I would hang sheets. One clothes pin could hold the end corner of one sheet and the beginning corner of another. This was called *over lapping*.

Once completed, we went back to wash the second load, the coloreds. This load was always the heaviest. Blankets, blue jeans, and towels made up the load and was always too heavy for me to handle once they were washed. So, DeeDee and Mom would put the washed load through the wringer to be rinsed.

Once the rays from the sun had dried the white clothes I would inform my mother, who then gave me permission to get the straw basket and start filling it with dry clothes. Meanwhile, DeeDee and Mom finished the second rinse and met me outside to hang the second load.

After all the laundry was dry, we sat in the kitchen and ate snacks. I listened to conversations between Mom and DeeDee as we folded clothes.

Each family members clothing had a designated, formatted position on the table. All Dads' socks were grouped and placed on the right side, along with his under garments and shirts, which soon had a destination with the iron. Mom shared the right side with Dad and my brothers shared the lower left side with me. The sheets were in a category of their own.

I was gleeful when it was time to fold sheets. I called them the "sheet monsters." I could have wrapped my frail body twice, maybe three times in them. However, when Mom and I took command of the corners, I was in charge. We would bring each of the assigned corners together and then meet in the middle to complete the task.

Yes, I had conquered the monster!

Putting them away in the drawer gave me assurance that the monster was buried.

After my great conquest, it was time for me to put my clothes in their assigned place and get ready for dinner.

Doing laundry with Mom and DeeDee was one of my fondest memories. I had assignments that assisted them with laundry day. I was asked to sort the colored cloths from the whites and the towels and wash cloths from the sheets. Another task of mine was to load the washing machine tube and empty it into straw baskets to be hung on the cloth lines outside. So much of my world was secluded by indoor isolation due to my eczema. Helping sort the clothes, fold the clothes and take them to their designated locations empowered me to believe that I was needed.

DeeDee and Mom would call my name to move the basket or check to see if the laundry outside was dry. They ran my little seventy-pound body until I was ready for an eight o'clock bedtime. After a day of doing the laundry, a good night sleep was welcomed!

*Marie Jenkins', My Time*

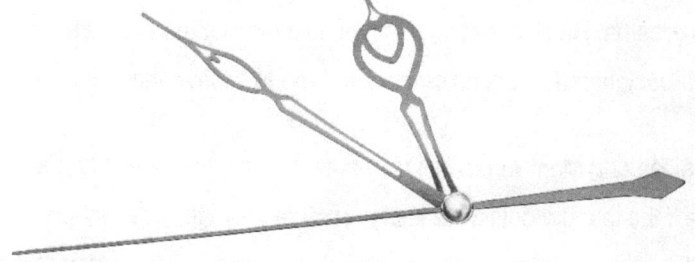

# Chapter Three: Storytime

*Little Marie*

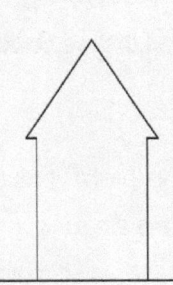

*I imagined the prince would come someday and rescue me from my pain. He would take me to his world where I would be cleansed once I reached the shores of a new day. A day that I could have many girlfriends having tea parties on the lawn of the castle. I imagined there would be girls from surrounding villages waiting for my invitation to join me in a day of play.*

My room was my sanctuary. As a result of my skin breakouts and scars, the safest place for me was my favorite room in the house, my bedroom. My doll babies shared space with me; they comforted me when I was not invited to join in outside games with the other children in the neighborhood. Rainy days were often welcomed by me as a relief to know that at least the others had to stay in as well.

My greatest joy was spending time with DeeDee. She occupied three rooms: the living room, a bedroom, and kitchen on the third floor of the house. To get to the third floor, there was a solid wood door at the bottom of a pair of steps that led to the destination.

Through the day, DeeDee kept that door closed.

*Marie Jenkins', My Time*

I was allowed to open the door and call for her and then wait until she asked, "Is that my little Marie?" Then I knew it was clear for me to climb the stairs that would bring me to a world of adventures.

DeeDee always had sugar cookies and milk set at *my* place at *her* kitchen table. I was always fascinated at the tile on the floor of the kitchen. It was checkerboard, black and white. I believed that we could play checkers, but we never did.

After the cookies and milk, DeeDee and I would settle in the living room, snuggled together on the settee, where she would tell me amazing stories of her childhood. After she finished her stories, she would motion for me to get a storybook from the credenza. This moment is what I anticipated. It was the crown and glory!

I would choose stories that allowed me to place myself within the pages of the books. I loved the story of *Red Riding Hood, Hansel and Gretel, Snow White* and *The Seven Dwarfs*. I pretended that I was the girl lying in the snow sleeping from the poisonous apple designed to keep me from my destiny. I imagined the prince would come someday and rescue me from my pain. He would take me to his world where I would be cleansed once I reached the shores of a new day. A day that I could have many girlfriends having tea parties on the lawn of the castle. I imagined there would be girls from surrounding villages waiting for my invitation to join me in a day of play.

Tiring from the visions in my head, I relaxed and tuned my ear to DeeDee's reading. As she read the individual stories, I would cuddle really close to her bosom, shut my eyes, and take the journey.

What seemed like only a moment had actually been hours.

When I opened my eyes from a comfortable nap, we were in another division of day. While I had been in slumber, DeeDee had placed the storybooks back where they belonged and finished cooking her dinner.

Once I gathered my thoughts, I arose, kissed her on the cheek thanked her for lunch and an adventurous afternoon.

"See you later gator," I announced sadly, "

"After while crocodile," DeeDee replied.

We exchanged, "I love you" and blew kisses as I moved from her sight down the steps.

*Marie Jenkins', My Time*

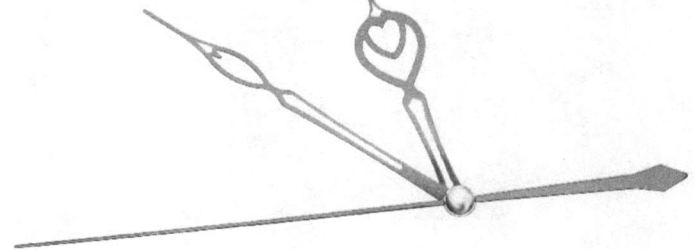

## Chapter Four: An Old Soul

*What the Night Reveals*

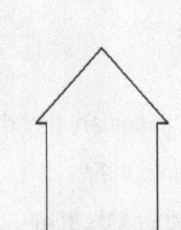

*I had begun to regress within myself. I built walls that kept me from feeling what others said about my condition. I hid the little girl who was being ostracized day in and day out. I sent her to a cocoon where I sang songs, had imaginary friends, and felt included.*

There were times of the year that were more favorable to me: fall, winter, and spring.

These seasons of the year it was more fashionable to wear layered clothing. However, when summer was in full bloom, I did not have the same options in my wardrobe as other girls my age. My selections of attire did not change much from season to season. Instead of tank tops, short sleeve shirts, and shorts, I wore long sleeve shirts and long pants. I preferred them because they hid my sores and my feelings of shame. I would peer from the living room window and see other girls wearing their cute summer outfits: sleeveless dresses, sandals, bobby socks and sneakers. I could not understand why I was cursed with this "skin disease."

I was so miserable inside and out! Some days the outside temperatures reached over ninety-degree Fahrenheit. Just sitting on the porch caused my body to sweat and itch uncontrollably. My clothing would stick to any open sores I had, causing increased pain and discomfort.

I compared myself to the lepers in the Bible who were outcast living in caves. They were disfigured, ostracized, and sentenced to live alone in their own shame and pain. I felt alone all my childhood.

My only friends were my doll babies, DeeDee, and the imaginary friends that I communed with. Storybook figures welcome me into their narratives. But I desired to have interactions with the other kids in my neighborhood.

After a series of food allergy tests, it was determined that I was having allergic reactions to food groups that produced citric acid, which were triggering allergic reactions. Dr. Farney hoped that by deceasing my diet of these acidic food groups, it would relieve the inflamed, cracked, red, rough, itchy reactions. Therefore, Dr. Farney (my Dermatologist) recommended that my mother place me on a non-citric, non-chocolate, non-caffeine diet in hopes that my blood would rid itself of the toxins caused by these food groups.

This became a nightmare I lived daily.

I was such a picky eater already. So, being denied chocolate candy, oranges, and soda was more than I could endure. I could no longer buy a Mello Cup or Reese Cup (two favorites from the Penny Candy Store). Nor could I celebrate Easter without a chocolate bunny, Christmas without a chocolate Santa, or delight in a Islay's chocolate ice cream cone. I felt that all parties involved had failed me.

*How could my mother and father agree to such torture for their only daughter!*

Temptations to indulge into prohibited moments of pleasure haunted me daily as I watched my brother, and his friends taunt me with mouthwatering chocolate candy bars. They were mean! They licked their dirty fingers in harmony as the last bite was devoured. Every eating action they made was directed toward me for the sake of their pleasure. They made plans for the next day and the day after that to replenish their chocolate stash from the corner store. The sight of my brother and the kids on our block delighting in pleasures that soothed their palate while mocking me with desire was overwhelming.

I wished the sky would have fallen in on all of them.

The boys even vowed to increase their appetites even the more with Hersey, Mounds, and Fifth Avenue bars. They tormented me day after day! My *sweets diet* was restricted to five flavors of hard candy, which I hated! None of the flavors were pleasing. None of the colors were appealing, and the red ones left a red sour taste and stained my tongue. I felt there was no future for me to live a normal life. I was doomed to a deprived life of desperation.

Alone, I would sneak to the corner store and buy a Reese Cup. Afterward, I would find an alley to hide away from my family. Sitting on the corner steps that led to an abandoned house I would indulge in the forbidden pleasure, chocolate! After every bite I would lick my lips and my hands, making certain that all was enjoyed. After most of these delightful experiences, night would tell the truth of what my day hid. I would scratch even more. Sometimes the episodes would be so severe until my God mother would sit at my bedside, rubbing and praying for my relief.

I could faintly hear her cries to God, as she sang, asking Him to heal me. When the song was silent, she would chant, speaking directly to God,

"Lord, please bless my little Marie," DeeDee chanted. "She's such a special child, chosen by you to fulfill your special purpose."

I wanted to believe that DeeDee had a divine connection with God, but I failed in my wanting when puss poured out of an open sore. DeeDee's prayers only made me sadder. I was convinced that God did not love me as much as my brother or any other child.

I hated myself! I hated that I had been born.

I had begun to regress within myself. I built walls that kept me from feeling what others said about my condition. I hid the little girl who was being ostracized day in and day out. I sent her to a cocoon where I sang songs, had imaginary friends, and felt included.

I prayed earnestly for a healing! I loved going to church. (Even when I was sick, I would cry if my dad left me home.) I did all I knew to do to be obedient. I could not understand why God was not hearing me.

Not only did I say my prayers each night asking Jesus to heal me, but the church also joined in with me, as well as family members. We all were desperately looking for a breakthrough, a scientific discovery, even a new serum injection, would have been welcomed.

Looking back, God did hear my prayers. The church members were the ones who accepted me just as I was. They never show any partiality between me and the other children. In fact, they poured so much love into my life. They knew I couldn't have chocolate candy, so they would bring me soft peppermint candy in a little brown paper bag. (To this day, I still love soft mints.) Some of the individually wrapped mints were stale, but I was always grateful and sucked on them harder until they dissipated on my palette.

I was a good girl. I was obedient. I participated in the children's choir, played the tambourine, helped the old ladies to their seats and assisted my father as much as I was given permission. I was an *old soul* due to my constant personal involvement with the senior citizens in my father's church, and the senior mothers at home.

Still, I was afflicted with sores from my head to my feet.

I was the child version of Job.

Restrictions, restrictions, restrictions consumed my being, from the clothes I wore, the food I ate, to the activities in which I was able to participate. There were those who would interact with me and those who would not.

Even family members would not have anything to do with me. My aunts did not even want me to hold their babies!

I was not only a loner, but I was alone.

# Chapter Five: David

*Answered Prayer*

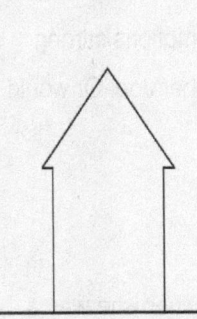

*There was something special about David! His personality lured one's affections towards him. While still only months old and before his first birthday, my mother and father took David to the doctor due to his continued crying and refusal to eat, irritability, and jaundiced skin. When they returned from the visit, we were given the devastating news, David had spinal meningitis.*

Twelve years after my birth, there was to be a new addition to our family. They planned to name the baby boy, David. A real live doll baby! I counted the days and nights when he would join the family. I assisted my dad in packing the suitcase with clothes for my mother and the baby to come home in from the hospital.

Finally, the day had arrived! My new brother was coming home. My feelings were aroused with joy and excitement. This was the day to meet the newest family member. My father named him after King David in the Bible.

The day dawned. After the cleansing of a spring shower, my dad pulled up to the house and parked. Puddles of water lined the sideway from the car to the steps of the porch. He turned off the ignition, opened his door, walked to the passenger's side, opened the door for my mom. I saw a blue blanket. But I couldn't see the baby. The blanket covered his head. My mother picked up the little package out of the car seat. From my position, it looked like an oblong parcel. As they entered the house, I was so excited! I wanted to see him. I had so many emotions stirring inside. I wondered if he would look like me or my brother Joe. Or would he look like some other family member.

*What color skin will he have?* I pondered.

My mother was fair skinned. She shared with us that when she was a little girl she was very light skinned with freckles and red hair. Whereas my dad's skin tone was chocolate brown.

Once in the house, my mother laid the blue bundle on the bed, still covered up. I could hear the small whimpering cries from beneath the blanket. My father helped my mother take her coat off for him to hang it up. Then she walked into the bathroom and washed her hands. Her actions seemed to take forever! By this time, my brother Joe, my God mother, and my aunt Mable had all gathered around the bed for the great reveal, I wanted to scream!

*Hurry up!*

In fear of what the repercussions would be, I held my tongue.

In one smooth movement, my mother un-wrapped the cover from baby David's face. I stood there in awe! His face was a reddish color from crying. His hands were very light with chocolate brown color around his fingernails and ears. His eyes were tightly shut. His little mouth and tongue were quivering. And a loud noise bellowed from his small body frame. His tiny hands were clinched expressing the uncertainty of his new surroundings.

I stayed focused as my mother gently un-wrapped the remaining portion of the blanket from around his body. Baby David was kicking and moving as he felt freedom. Everyone wanted to hold him. Before any of us could get our wish to hold him, we all had to make a trip to the bathroom. We had a handwashing service. I was the last in line. By this time, baby David was tired and hungry. After he consumed his eight ounces of milk and burped, my mother laid him down in the crib. It wasn't long after, David was sleeping peacefully. My mother went to the kitchen to prepare his formula of equal parts of Karo syrup (light), Carnation milk and boiled water. This formula was prescribed by the pediatrician. This formula was tried and true, which was passed down to me, and I used it for my children.

I would run back and forth, checking on David, and watching my mother prepare the bottles for the baby. Everything had to be boiled, sterilized and prepared special. He even had a special shelf in the cabinet. He had his own dresser drawer, soap powder, boiling pot, baby spoon, and a food dish divided into three sections. In the bottom of the dish, hot water was retained to keep the baby food warm.

The second time I checked on baby David, he had facial movements. He yawned, smiled in his sleep, and wrinkled his face from discomfort. I discovered that the discomfort was relieved when he passed gas. I giggled with amusement.

There was something special about David! His personality lured one's affections towards him. While still only months old and before his first birthday, my mother and father took David to the doctor due to his continued crying and refusal to eat, irritability, and jaundiced skin. When they returned from the visit, we were given the devastating news, David had spinal meningitis.

That evening was Friday night church service. Everyone was required to attend, even David.

My parents wrapped him in his blanket, placed him in the car seat and started a silent, sad travel to 3412 Ligionier Street, Pittsburgh, Pa., church. After my father preached the sermon, he made an altar call for anyone who wanted to give their life to Jesus Christ.

Within the same sentence he "opened the doors of the church" to anyone who would desire to become a member. He then called for my mother to bring David to the altar. He asked for a few drops of anointing oil in the palms of his hands. He instructed my mother to put David in his arms. Upon doing so, he anointed David's head with oil and asked the saints to join him in prayer, as he made his request before the Lord.

There was much rejoicing that night as my father and the congregation believed that the Lord heard their cries and delivered baby David from his infirmity.

I cannot remember exactly when the healing occurred, but I do know that when my parents took David back to the Doctor for a follow-up, the tests came back negative!

God had granted my father and the congregation's prayer request to heal David.

Photo 3: Our beloved David

*Marie Jenkins', My Time*

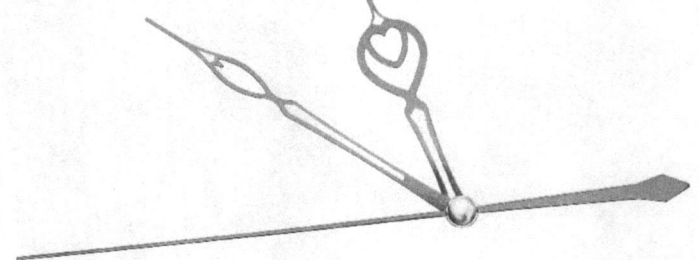

# Chapter Six: Master of The Pots

*What Do We Do Now?*

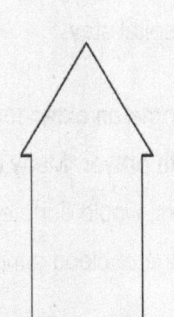

*Little did we know, David had already transitioned. He did not make it. I was numb. I could hear my heart beating in my thoughts. I did not know how to console my mother or my sister-n-law. I was lost in the moment. The events that led to that moment began to replay over and over in my mind. Then for a short time, I lost all existence of reality.*

*My brother's passing was my first real experience with death.*

Years later David was diagnosed with Sickle Cell Anemia. He became our Apostle Paul who sought the Lord three times regarding the thorn in his side. The Lord responded to my brother David, as he did to the apostle Paul, "My grace is sufficient for you." **2 Corinthians 12:9 KJV**

With the grace of God, the support of my family, and the prayers of the saints, David was able to graduate high school and pursue his desire of becoming a chef. Friends of my parents owned a Restaurant and Banquet Hall. They were inspired by David's story of survival. They had a culinary program that David enrolled in. He was thrilled at the opportunity, living his dream. He had become quite the *master of the pots*. His fried chicken was second to none. Collard greens, corn bread, along with taking command of the grill had become his trademark.

This success did not come without health challenges. Often, he was stricken with excruciating pain from the decease of cycle cell anemia. My heart would hurt for him because when the attacks came, he would have to have a blood transfusion which required a hospital stay.

Our family along with those who loved him would become an extended part of his health care. We rallied around the clock with prayer. Many of the members of our church, along with family members, would donate blood in advance for David. There was never a shortage of blood supply for him. My family was so grateful for their sacrifices.

As soon as David was released from the hospital the next day he would be back on his post, wearing a chef hat and apron. The owners of the *Southern Platter* restaurant were kind and understanding regarding David's illness. They never held his absenteeism against him. He was treated with the same respect and requirements as the other employees. He was even given a weekly stipend while in training and extra pay when he prepared a Banquet event. This gave him a sense of manly pride.

David saved his money. But he also, bought clothing outfits. He met a young lady that he fell in love with. David was able to take her on dates and pay for the expenses. Soon after their meeting, perhaps a year, they were married by my father.

What a celebration!

David's life was as normal as God allowed. He was so happy. He still had episodes with his illness and the family was extremely concerned how his new wife would handle his suffering. But our concerns quickly faded, as she continued to remain by his side, even when he had to endure a hospital stay.

I remember the day of his transition from this life as if it were yesterday.

I received a phone call from my mother that David had been taken to a hospital in Pittsburgh as a request from her. My mother felt that David would receive better care and the reserved blood supply was also available in their facility. What we did not anticipate was that would be the last time we would have a conversation with him.

When I arrived at the hospital and entered his room, he looked drained from the ordeal of pain, blood transfusion, needles, tests, and constant medical probing. We were glad to see each other! We had a conversation and I caught him up on all the latest.

He was so excited about becoming a father. My sister-n-law was about six months pregnant and beginning to show signs of a protruding bulge from her stomach. The entire family was excited!

Our conversation was interrupted by the entrance of two nurses who were instructed to change David's bedding and hospital gown. We were politely asked to leave the room while they were going to start the process of changing the linen, redressing David, and doing a little housekeeping.

I remember David's face and words to us as if it were yesterday. He was reaching for us with the hand that was not attached to an I.V. drip and begged us not to leave. His eyes were glossy with tears, his voice was raspy with fear, "Please don't leave me. I won't be here when you come back."

We all tried to console him against his fears. This only aggravated him which elevated the tone in his voice as he insisted that he would not be there when we returned.

Our family was in disarray.

The nurses where impatiently starring, waiting for us to comply with *their* request as we tried to make sense of *David's* request.

*Did he think they were going to hurt him?* I thought.

I was so confused in my judgment! In a moment, I decided to stand in the doorway to still have immediate access to David just in case he cried out for help. When we stepped out the nurse drew the curtain and asked that I stand back from the entrance of the door. When I stepped back, she closed the door.

My emotions were all over the place. I felt anger, insulted, and disrespected. At that point I took charge of the conversation between family members regarding asserting authority over the situation. Just as I was about to act upon my decision to reenter the room, the nurse opened the door and invited the family to return.

David was now sleeping peacefully.

Or so we thought. Little did we know, David had already transitioned. He didn't make it. I was numb. I could hear my heart beating in my thoughts. I did not know how to console my mother or my sister-n-law. I was lost in the moment. The events that led to that moment began to replay over and over in my mind. Then for a short time, I lost all existence of reality.

My brother's passing was my first *real* experience with death.

*What do we do now?* I kept asking myself.

But I had no answer.

My father was never the same after the death of David.

Individually, we mourned. I believe it was too painful to speak about David as a family.

With the help of the Lord, we began to rebuild our lives without him. We were in preparation for new life to be born. She was a beautiful baby girl, David's daughter.

She will always be a reminder of his existence.

*Marie Jenkins', My Time*

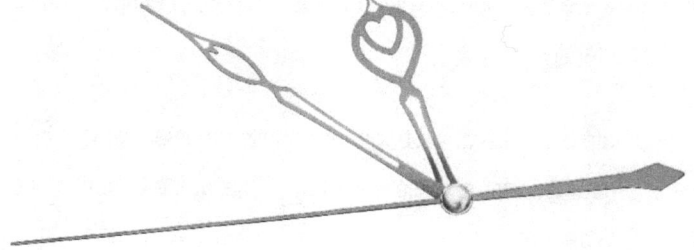

## Chapter Seven: Michael

*A Withdrawal into Silence*

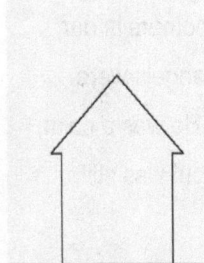

*Death permanently separates relationships without civility.*

*It robs the future of what could have been.*

*It freezes time to thought, recalled, and remembered.*

Two years and eight months after the birth of my brother David, a new arrival joined the family, his name was Michael.

When my mother brought him home from the hospital, he was tightly wrapped in a blue blanket that also covered his face. After my mother laid him on the bed, she began to dis-robe his blanket. Underneath, baby Michael was dressed in a light blue sweater set, that displayed a matching skull cap and booties with stings running along the outer edges of the bootie and tied with dangling blue pom poms.

When his cap was removed, it unveiled beautiful jet-black, curly hair.

He was so cute.

Amazingly, Michael slept throughout the whole ordeal. My mother placed him in the crib that had once belonged to David. Now, it had a new resident. I sat on the edge of the bed, peering through the slats of the crib, watching baby Michael sleep. He produced various facial expressions. Sometimes he would smile, while his hand would flinch. And other times he would toot out his lower lip with discomfort. I was fascinated by his body language. Some of the other mothers in our church would comment that when a baby smiles, the angels were playing with them. They must have loved my brother. He was a calm, pleasant little soul. He never cried as much as David but was still interesting to watch.

Later, as the two of them grew, conflict sometimes arose. As with any siblings there was tension between the two of them, as well. Disruptions over toy ownership that generally had to be settled by my parents. Most of the time Michael won the debate because of his status in the family, he was the baby. Despite sibling rivalry, there was a bond of love between them. They had become two peas in a pod, Batman and Robin, Frick and Frack, Fred and Barney.

My father purchased a metal outdoor play gym for us. There were two swings, a sliding board, a jungle gym, and a two-seat playset that swung back and forth.

We were the envy of the neighborhood!

Everyone wanted to be our friend, so they could have access to our treasure. My brothers and I spent hours playing on the gym. I would push David and Michael on the swings. For some odd reason, they just could not seem to get their legs to pump them on their own. Both would cry out, "push me higher." They both were competing, as to who could reach the sky first.

The back yard was large and accommodating. We were able to play dodge ball, baseball, and kick ball. When the neighborhood children would join us, we would pick teams for the challenge. I would always be a team captain. David and Michael would be team members. Because they were still little guys, my oldest brother Joe would kick the ball or hit the ball and David, or Michael would run the bases.

We were a fierce and dominating force!

For the most part, we won! If the other team from the neighborhood won, we would give them permission to use our play gym. Oh, did they feel privileged! Usually, while they were occupied on the play gym with Joe, I would take David and Michael for a ride in the red wagon. My father bought David a wagon one year for Christmas. He loved that wagon. They both could fit in it, with David in the back and Michael sitting in between his legs.

"Hold on," I would tell them as I ran up and down our front sidewalk.

David would wrap his little arms around Michael's small waist, squeezing, giggling, and screaming with joy. I would run my young legs off to make them happy. When I could no longer force my legs to obey the demands of their request to run, I would return the wagon back to the house, around to the back yard, and fall out on grass filled from exhaustion and laughter.

The death of David hit Michael, extremely hard.

He never really expressed his feelings, yet you could see the sadness in his persona. His eyes told the story of grieving a brother.

Death permanently separates relationships without civility.

It robs the future of what could have been.

It freezes time to thought, recalled, and remembered.

I never witnessed Michael's tears, although I saw his withdrawal into silence.

Without words, without David, we pushed through our pain, together.

## Chapter Eight: Life

*No Place Like Home*

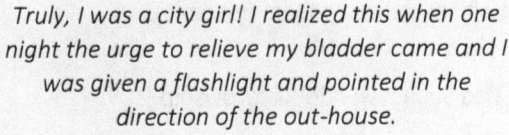

*Truly, I was a city girl! I realized this when one night the urge to relieve my bladder came and I was given a flashlight and pointed in the direction of the out-house.*

*Just getting to the out-house became a strategic, military plan.*
*Running was the best option!*

*Snakes, crickets, mosquitos, owls, bats, and creatures that were un-identifiable to me were all possibilities. I didn't know much, but what I did know was that they were the possessors of the land.*

At the tender age of eighteen, I was already married with a baby and making plans to join my husband in Germany.

The plan was to fly from Pittsburgh International Airport into New York's, LaGuardia Airport. An aunt who lived in Brooklyn had agreed that my son Ronnie and I could stay with her for three days until we could board our connecting, final flight to Frankfort, Germany.

Upon my announcement of my impending departure, my mother along with family and church members hosted a bon voyage party to celebrate my journey. Everyone brought their best dishes: casseroles, pound cakes, sweet potato and lemon meringue pies. Some of my aunts prepared old family recipes of potato salad, macaron and cheese, string beans, and my mother's all-time favorite was present: a lime green jello ring with sliced cucumbers (yummie).

We had such a wonderful fellowship.

I passed around pictures of Europe that Ronnie Sr. (my husband) had sent me, while expressing my overwhelming excitement! For most of the event, my mother held on to her grandson, who had become attached to her as well.

The evening ended with hugs, kisses, well wishes, and prayers of protection from God.

It did not take me long to pack. Most of the wedding gifts Ronnie Sr. and I received (blankets, sheet sets, towels and wash cloths, pots and pans, silverware, mugs and glassware) were previously shipped. I had to make sure heavy clothing was included in my luggage. Ronnie Sr. continued to remind me of the cold blistering weather in the winter months. He referred the blowing winds of Germany as *The Hawk*.

Later, after I experienced their winter storms, it certainly earned the reference because the wind would flap its breeze with a gliding pattern crisscrossing continuously without humor or regret. The wind attacks would continue, maneuvering fast, sweeping low, until the prey would yield to its treacherous overtures. The winds were in total control of the prey. They would take your breath away, cause your body to believe it was indifferent, rendering it unable to think, feel, or react normally.

There was only one thought: *How do I escape!*

Without a plan, you would be seduced and forced to succumb to its overwhelming massiveness.

A few days before the journey, I took little Ron to visit with Ronnie Sr.'s parents, uncles, and aunts. As part of the family, we were invited on Sundays after church, to join the family at the dining room table for a *soul food* dinner.

Soul food was the cuisine of the day: Collard greens, corn bread, southern fried chicken, potato salad, fried okra, homemade biscuits, string beans, smoked neckbones, homemade pound cake and sweet potato pie.

*Did I forget to mention freshly made lemonade?*

I still laugh at the stories that were shared across the table. Each family member could not wait for their turn. I often wondered if some stories were either embellished or downright fictitious. Nevertheless, they were amusing!

The joyful mood of the afternoon began to fade into sadness when the conversation shifted to mine and little Ron's impending departure to Germany. Even though the temperature of everyone's heart's folly diminished lower into a solemn reality of sadness, we managed to find humor as we discussed the dramatic lifestyle change that awaited us.

Departing from my in-laws overwhelmed my emotions. I began to tear-up, while my heart became joyless. I assured them that I would send pictures, often. Then with little Ron, I returned to my parent's home to prepare for more goodbyes.

I was young at the time so while there was a measure of sadness over leaving the familiarity of family and friends, I was also excited about experiencing a new country and culture. As I reflect on it now, I realize there is an unnatural innocence that accompanies youth.

Packing our clothes with glee and contentment, I was sure to pack pictures from the farewell party. They would remind me of those I would be temporarily leaving behind.

Most of the church members had given me what they referred to as "a token of love" or money and I had already had an appointment with the branch office Bank in my community to convert the cash to Travelers Checks. I checked my 'to do' list twice over to make sure I was taking everything that I would need to be able to live in comfort in Germany.

Little Ron's immunizations and vaccinations where up to date, as well as mine, for traveling outside the country. I prepared a small bag with cough syrups, Vicks Vapor Rubs, Baby Aspirins, noise and eye drops, Vaseline, Baby Shampoo and soap, toothbrush/paste, mouthwash, lotions, bath bubbles, and Chap Stix for the journey. I was covering all the bases!

Having said my goodbyes to the church congregation and extended family, what was left was the arduous task of leaving my mother. Our bond and now the attachment she had with my son (a bond to be admired) caused me to momentarily agonize over leaving.

I knew that for both little Ron and my mother, the coming days would be nearly unbearable. Their morning routine would be interrupted. Mother always retrieved him from his crib for his first feeding despite her resistance to being an early riser.

My emotions were all over the place. I was giddy with excitement yet sadden by the fact that I would not be in fellowship with my family. My parents would not experience the excitement of Ron's first Christmas. Nor would they have the pleasure of witnessing his participation in the Easter Parade. I made a specific heart note to take pictures of these two events from Germany to share with the family.

The next morning reiterated the positivity of reality: little Ron and I were on our way to Germany!

Our luggage was lined up neatly by the front door, ready to be placed in the trunk of the car. Before my father went to work, he placed the luggage in my mother's car. My mother was not an experienced highway diver, therefore, to take us to the Pittsburgh International Airport would have been a grueling experience for her. She did offer to take us to downtown Pittsburgh to the Bus Station to catch the airport bus.

Before we drove off, my father prayed a prayer of protection for me and the baby. He hugged us both with closing words of comfort. As he was pulling out from in front of the house, Ron and I was getting into the car with my mother. Although, I was excited about the trip, I felt a wave of sadness. I had never been without my family. Everything that I knew about life revolved around my family, church, school, growing up, friends, and my brothers. I could only remember three instances where I had traveled outside of this comfort zone.

The first time I left the neighborhood is when my father took my oldest brother and I to see our cousins who lived in the country, about a thirty miles drive. That first trip seemed like it took forever to get there. I was so fascinated with country living, I wanted to spend a summer. Well, little did I know, my parents gave me permission the following summer to spend a week with those same cousins. I strongly suggested that was a gross mistake for me.

Truly, I was a city girl! I realized this when one night the urge to relieve my bladder came and I was given a flashlight and pointed in the direction of the *out-house*.

Just getting to the out-house became a strategic, military plan. Running was the best option!

Snakes, crickets, mosquitos, owls, bats, and creatures that were unidentifiable to me were all possibilities. I didn't know much, but what I did know was that *they* were the possessors of the land.

After the first night, I called my parents and begged my father to come and get me!

He did, but only after the week was over.

The second experience was more pleasurable.

A Pastor and his wife (who were good friends with my parents), asked if my brother and I could attend the Pennsylvania State Fair. To our surprise, my parents said, "Yes." The couple picked us up around five o'clock in the morning. The sun had not rose from the night skies. The feeling was exhilarating as we watched and welcomed the sun rise over the horizon.

Again, I felt it was a road trip that lasted forever.

Finally, we reached the destination.

As the day progressed, evening settled in with its cool breeze. I became weary and cold. My feet were hurting! I wanted to go home. I had had enough of the stinky animals and rides on the Ferris Wheel. I was not interested in milking cows, chasing oinking pigs, gathering eggs from the cages of hens, or trying to catch a chicken.

My thoughts were, *Take me back to the city!*

In my third experience away from home, I was with my God mother (DeeDee), her sister and husband.

Early one Saturday morning, DeeDee's sister and brother-in-law picked us up from my parents' house and we embarked on roads that would take us to their summer home. Yes, you guessed it - in the country. Deep in the country!

Their home was the only house for miles and miles. They had animals much like the state fair: chickens, pigs, cows, a horse, two dogs, and a cat. Mrs. Thornton (DeeDee's sister) canned jelly, fruit, string beans, carrots, and other foods that I could not rightly identify. She froze freshly baked breads, cakes, and cookies. They churned butter and skimmed the fat from off the top of the milk. The best was the homemade vanilla ice cream. Mrs. Thornton gave me permission to turn the handle of the ice bucket where the ingredients lined the bottom.

Often Mr. Thornton would put crushed ice and rock salt in the top. He said that helped to form the ice cream.

As good as that ice cream was, again I found myself yearning to return to the city. When night fell, you could not see your hand in front of your face! Sitting on the porch that wrapped around the house with only hurricane candles offering light, the night creatures appeared with speed.

Finally, we packed the car with canned foods, breads, freshly baked pound cake, and homemade jelly to take back for God mother DeeDee to share with my mother.

*Did I mention Mrs. Thornton also made homemade soap?*

It was put in the box as well.

I prayed Germany would not be country.

Mother delivered little Ron and I safely to the bus station. While removing the luggage from the trunk of the car, I noticed tears in my mother's eyes. She was holding little Ron, gripping him gently and with affection told him how much she loved and would miss him.

After several face kisses, she passed him back to my awaiting arms.

She and I exchanged good-byes, love yous, hugs and kisses.

A Porter assisted me with our luggage as we walked into the bus station. I looked back and saw my mother standing there watching us as we would eventually disappear from her gaze.

*Marie Jenkins', My Time*

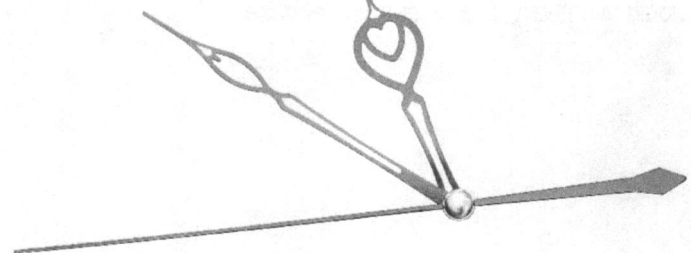

# Chapter Nine: Life

*A Real-Life Fairytale*

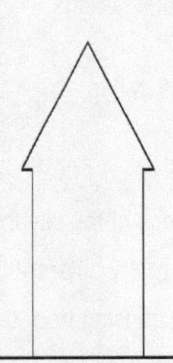

> Looking out the window of the cab unveiled the opulence of the city that never sleeps, New York. I was in awe! There were so many different things to see – all taking place at once. My eyes were dancing from one position to another. By this time little Ron was sleeping, cuddled in my arms. My aunt was proudly telling me about the pulse of the Big Apple. I was absorbing her dialog while inserting questions about her neighborhood, the diversity of nationalities, China town, Harlem, and the famous Apollo theater.

I sat in the terminal with my baby waiting for the announcement. Finally, I heard over the speaker that the bus leaving for Brooklyn, New York was ready to receive ticket holders. The same Porter placed our luggage in the bottom of the bus. Entering the bus was a tantalizing experience. My emotions were all over the place. I was verbally sharing the experience with Ron. I felt so grown up! I was doing this on my own. I was not encumbered with anxiety or fear.

Perhaps, like most young people, I felt the world was my oyster.

Around eight hours later, the driver announced that we were pulling into Brooklyn's bus terminal. From the window I could see my aunt waiting for our arrival. As I exited the bus, I noticed the Porter had placed our luggage on a baggage cart. I embraced my aunt with joy and a *glad to see you!*

She took little Ron in her arms, bathing him with kisses and hugs.

Eventually, my aunt hailed a Gypsy cab to transport us to her apartment.

Looking out the window of the cab unveiled the opulence of the city that never sleeps, New York. I was in awe! There were so many different things to see – all taking place at once. My eyes were dancing from one position to another. By this time little Ron was sleeping, cuddled in my arms. My aunt was proudly telling me about the pulse of the Big Apple. I was absorbing her dialog while inserting questions about her neighborhood, the diversity of nationalities, China town, Harlem, and the famous Apollo theater.

As soon as she answered one question, I had ten more to explore.

Later, after the baby was put to bed for the night, I continued to talk with my aunt over a hot cup of tea. She not only enlightened me with New York history, she shared intimate family stories regarding my aunts, uncle, and my mother and father. I was fascinated when she told me the love story of how my mother and father met, dated, became engaged and eventually married.

"Your father was a very handsome man. He had a boyish charm and compelling smile. And he was tall," my aunt said and whistled. "Six feet I know. And with your mama only being five feet tall, he towered over her like a tree."

We laughed at that.

"I'll never forget the first time she brought him by to meet us all. Those slender, broad shoulders and smooth chocolate skin had us all fanning our faces," she laughed again. "And when he opened his mouth to introduce himself, his deep baritone voice shook the room. Your mama said she always knew he was going to be a preacher because of his voice. She said his voice demanded attention."

My aunt was right. My father's voice was impressive. He did not have to shout.

"The night he proposed, I knew it before she did."

"You did," I asked, feeling like the little girl who sat in anticipation as DeeDee read fairytale romance stories. Only this one was real.

"I sure did," my aunt said. "He showed up in a three-piece blue pin stripe suit, wing tip shoes, gold cuff links and a gold pocket watch hanging off the vest of his suit!"

"Ooooh," I shouted and then clamped my hand over my mouth. I did not want to wake little Ron. "Daddy was sharp."

"He sure was. Now your mama didn't look too bad herself. She may have been short, but them beautiful curvy legs, sandy red hair, and pleasing light brown skin never left her wanting for attention," my aunt said with the pride only a big sister would have. "My sister's waist was all of twenty-three inches. She was a doll baby for sure!"

"Anyway," my aunt continued as she poured us a second cup of tea. "When your father pulled up in that Model T, Ford dressed like he was, I knew that he planned to take our dear sister away from us."

Their story resembled Cinderella with exception of my mother returning the glass slipper to my father when she was angry at my father (smile). My aunt told me several stories that night that my mother had shared with her.

We stayed up into the wee hours of the morning. Finally, my eyes began to close and just like I did during Storytime with DeeDee, I soon fell asleep nestled next to my aunt. Sleep felt so good on my tired, exhausted body.

I did not stir until the next morning when I awoke the next morning on my aunt's couch covered with a blanket to the cries of little Ron, looking for his mother and breakfast.

# Chapter Ten: Germany

*A Flash of Life*

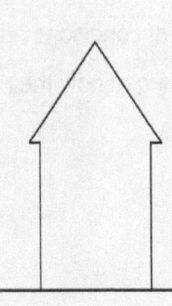

In a moment, my life flashed before me. The good, bad, and ugly. I was entering into a different culture, a world where I did not know anyone except my husband. I trusted him for being my leader and guide as we settled into our new lifestyle. I believed in him to be my problem solver, strong in the face of adversity, able to navigate complex situations that would benefit our health and well-being.

After breakfast, I dressed little Ron and I for the day. Then we waited for my aunt to return.

When I looked out the bedroom window, I was truly amazed at the surroundings. The bedroom window faced the back of the apartment, which formed a courtyard with the connecting buildings. All the windows were symmetrically lined across from each other.

The laundry system here at my aunt's apartment, while similar to ours, was significantly different. A rope-like contraption was attached to each occupant's window forming a clothing line. I later learned that tenants were assigned a laundry day to ensure that each resident had a fair opportunity using the pully system to hang and dry their laundry.

Wet clothes were one by one pinned on the line and then using the pully system, hand maneuvered to advance to the next section. I was so fascinated!

Down below parents could watch their children play in the play-yard.

I understand that each community had its own system of conditions and limitations of existence. The neighborhood had a *knowing* of how their set-up worked and an expectation of conformity.

Finally, I heard the key turn the lock.

My aunt emerged saying, "Are you ready to go?"

I answered with glee, "Yes!"

After calling for a gypsy cab (private contractors who operated their own car service) we headed to our destination of West Broadway, Soho to experience blocks and blocks of vendors. I was overwhelmed by the noise and movement of the people. The streets were loaded with bodies. This would be the first time I ate food from a vendor truck. We stopped at one for lunch. I ordered a hot sausage sandwich (with extra onions and green peppers) and a coke. The sandwich was supersized. The sausage extended beyond the bun. As I requested, they sauteed the onions and green peppers. Some were sliding down the side of the bun. I ate as much as my stomach could hold.

Further along the sidewalk were vendors selling children's clothing. I purchase a few outfits for little Ron. The day was dissolving into evening. As dusk announced its arrival, my legs and arms were tired; and little Ron was fussy. It was time to return to Brooklyn.

I started repacking that night for the flight to Germany. The flight was scheduled for morning. My aunt and I spent the remaining evening rekindling the day and surmising how I thought our lives would be in Germany. After playing with little Ron, my aunt laid his head on her breast, rocking him to sleep.

It seemed like I had just laid my head on the pillow, when I woke to the sound of my aunt's voice, telling me it was time to get up. We needed to arrive to JFK airport on time for our flight.

I was so excited!

I did not have a sense of fear or anguish but was instead stimulated by thoughts of grandeur. Again, my aunt called for a gypsy cab. Soon we were on our way. Traffic was so congested. People were honking their horns; others were cutting in and out of lanes causing some drivers to give them the middle finger. All this excitement just to get to a location.

Finally, we were at the drop off point of JFK airport. Hugs and kisses were exchanged, and I thanked Aunt Mary for her hospitality and kindness. I assured her I would call when I reached the Frankfurt airport as well as send her something special from Germany to add to her *nicknack* collection. Swollen with excitement, after kissing my aunt and saying good-by and waving Ron's little hand in mine to her, we watched as the gypsy cab driver drive off. Then we entered the airport, prepared to board the 757.

I had never seen an airport so large!

It looked like a city inside a cubicle. After checking our luggage, I asked for directions where to board the plane. The lady not only told me; she was kind enough to escort us to the Security check point. The wait was extremely long, and little Ron had begun to be restless. After what seemed to be forever, I was beckoned to step up and produce our Passport and boarding ticket. The Security Guard matched our faces with the picture on the passport and asked if our trip was for business or pleasure. I answered with too much information. I gave him the history for our travel.

He stamped the passport saying, "Enjoy your husband and your stay."

Down a long cold corridor was the entrance to the waiting room for boarding. There was enough time before boarding for us to have breakfast. I spotted a vendor advertising breakfast and purchased food. After we finished, I found a seat and waited for the call to board the plane. Ron was being occupied by the cartoons on one of the tv monitors.

Then it was time. I heard the stewardess call for our non-stop flight to Frankfort, Germany. We boarded a Lufthansa airline, Boeing 747 that was longer than a football field and wider than our neighborhood, or so it seemed. We were pointed to a window seat in the middle of the plane. We each had our own seats. I buckled us in according to the instructions given by the airline stewardess. Finally, after all the safety instructions, we were pulling onto the runway. At first, we were taxing and then, we were moving at a tremendously high rate of speed. I watched in awe as the plane began to elevate upwards into the sky. Soon we were over the clouds. I experienced peace, claim and tranquility. The sun was shining with such grace and dignity. Little Ron was too young to appreciate flying over the rainbow. So, I just relaxed and ingested the ambience.

I was wakened by the airplane stewardess with lunch and dinner menu choices. After my selections lunch was served. I plugged in our earphones, Ron watched cartoons and I selected a movie, which passed the time. We both took a nap and again was awaken to the serving of dinner being distributed. As we settled into night fall, I adjusted our seats to reflect lounge chairs. The rest was not well for me. Some passengers were snoring, others were walking around engaged in disturbing conversations. Others were weary from the loss of sleep.

Finally, the speaker announced that we were not far from landing. Breakfast was being served. I needed caffeine, badly. Hours passed when the pilots voice filled the plane with the instructions to, "Fasten your seat belts. We are just waiting for the signal from Air Traffic Control to tell us to proceed to descend to the runway for landing."

My heart skipped a beat. We had arrived in Germany!

I immediately thanked the Lord for safe travels.

I was so excited to see my husband. I did not know if little Ron would remember his father as he was still an infant when Ron Sr. left for the Army. Little Ron was named after his father, but he was not a junior. His middle name was the same as his grandfather, Ron Sr's dad.

Once we landed, the plane taxied for some time before the pilot pulled into the gate.

In a moment, my life flashed before me. The good, bad and ugly. I was entering into a different culture, a world where I did not know anyone except my husband. I trusted him for being my leader and guide as we settled into our new lifestyle. I believed in him to be my problem solver, strong in the face of adversity, able to navigate complex situations that would benefit our health and well-being.

As I witnessed the stewardess prepare for our disembark from the plane, there were bells ringing at three pitch levels, requiring everyone's attention. The pilot cheerfully informed all passengers of a safe landing. He further thanked everyone for choosing Lufthansa airline, Boeing 747 as their transportation. He politely expressed his gratitude, making it known to the other pilots and stewardess, who were also smiling and waving goodbye, and agreed, for our trust and cooperation. He welcomed us to use Lufthansa airlines for future travel. A second series of bells rang, the overhead lights came on, and we were instructed to be patient for the unloading of passengers.

# Chapter Eleven: Visions

*Grandeur and Nightmares*

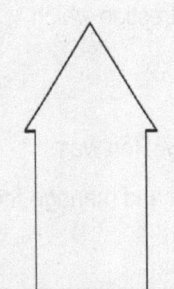

*My husband and I were alone. He tried to avoid me and all the questions that I demanded answers to. We argued just about all night until I had only a whimper of a voice. At that moment, I felt as if I hated him. I shipped household goods, as well as extra money so when we arrived, foundational necessities would already be in place. He had spent the money and the household goods where in storage on his base.*

We reached our destination within a one night's sleep. Little Ron was getting restless. While trying to entertain him, gathering our luggage from the overhead bin, my emotions were all over the place. I was excited, nervous, and afraid. Whenever my emotions would become agitated, my eczema would flair up and I would begin to scratch.

I was scratching so hard; I could feel the trinkle of blood oozing from my skin.

It was time for our row to exit. Little Ron and I waved to the staff and walked through the long tube that led into the airport. I was earnestly looking for my husband. After scanning the crowd without recognition of him, tears formed in my eyes.

"Where are family members located?" I asked one of the airport workers. She pointed to the signs that were in several different languages. "But first, you need to collect your carryon luggage." I did as she suggested and then she pointed me in the right direction which included down escalators and long halls.

My heart was racing with every step of my foot journey. Ron was cranky, fussy, and hungry. While trying to console him and manage the luggage from the plane, I wanted to cry. I needed help!

Finally, a luggage worker asked if he could be of any assistance?

I responded, "Yes!" He led us to the correct terminal where the remainder of our luggage could be retrieved. After he loaded our suitcases on the cart, he guided us through the tunnel where we could connect with loved ones who were waiting for the arrivals of family and friends. As I got closer to the end of the ramp, I saw him, my husband! I was so excited; I began grinning from ear to ear. I began bouncing little Ron up and down, while sharing with him, "There is Daddy."

I was moving so quickly until I left the baggage worker behind. As he caught up with us, both little Ron and I were in a group hug embrace with Ron Sr. After my husband tipped the worker, we were introduced to his Army Sergeant. (We will call him, Jim.) Jim was huge in statue, fair skinned, over sizable in weight, tall and towering in height, with a smile that would drop New York's New Year's crystal ball with the electricity that illuminated from his face.

I remember at that moment; I was so happy to meet him. Surely, he was a friend.

I held little Ron while Ron Sr. and Jim loaded the luggage into the army jeep. I was signaled to get into the back, Ron held his namesake on the passenger' side, while Jim slowly and carefully drove from the airport terminal. I immediately noticed the drop in temperature. It was cold! I was hesitant to ask, "Could the heat be turned up?"

I figured out the coldness I was experiencing was normal to them. So, I rode in cold silence.

Little Ron was warm and cozy in his snow suit.

Riding through the city of Frankfort reminded me of New York. There were bright lights that framed and invited all to join celebrations of fine dining, shopping, or a night out on the town. I was fascinated with the couture of fashions. Lots and lots of cloth layering and fur coats, hats, gloves, boots, and collars to guard one's flesh.

Finally, after what seemed to be a trip cross country to grandma house, we reached the small, quaint town of Wildflicken.

I had so many visions of grandeur in my thoughts. For the next twelve to eighteen months, I would watch little Ron grow, form new relationships, learn how to navigate around town, seek out the best areas where toddlers could play in a park in spring and summer, and enjoy being a mother and wife. Little Ron would experience his first bicycle, playing catch with his father.

At last, we pulled up to the apartment building. Peering out of the window, it looked like a warehouse with windows on the second and third floors. The bottom of the building had one entrance door and one full pane window on the right facing the building. Underneath the window was a flower box. The length of the pot extended across the entire bottom of the window. All vegetation was dead due to the inclement weather. It was a brick building with the entire first story covered with a smooth concrete finish. Which gave me the impression that it was a warehouse.

Not very inviting nor appealing.

Reality asked, *Is this where you will be staying for your European experience? What kind of pictures would you possibly possible send back home to boast of a proud residency?*

When I refocused the present situation, little Ron had been given back to me. Ron Sr. and Jim were unloading luggage and placing them at the front door. They signaled to me to remove myself from the vehicle as they made their way up a flight of steps where there were two apartments from doors opposite each other. When Jim unlocked the door on the left side of the hall, I could relax in our apartment. I was confident that he would precede on to his apartment across the hall. I was sure we would be neighbors. I was out done when the luggage was placed in his hallway. I thought surely there must be a mistake. Then we were greeted by his wife (Nancy) and son (Billy) who appeared to be a couple months older than my son. Nancy was kind and gracious as she ushered us into their living space. Billy wanted to play, but little Ron was withdrawn and unapologetic to his advances. Now he was crying as I tried to comfort him.

I caught the eye of my husband and starred at him with disbelief and horror!

Surely, this was a temporary situation!

I could read the expression on Nancy's face who knew that I was not happy or comfortable with this arrangement. Our luggage was piled inside in a small room. I could not see the contents of the room because the light was off. Nancy took our outer garments, hung them up in the hallway and offered hot chocolate to all of us as we gathered in the dining room to fellowship.

I was so hurt, disappointed, and angry. I fought back the tears that threatened to fall down my cheeks. My emotions were raging, and my skin was taking a beating. After a few sips of hot chocolate, I was told that we were spending the night. I was furious!

I was not used to sharing living space with anyone else other than my parents.

When I turned on the light in the designated room, I became nauseated by its contents. The room measurement could not have been more than a twelve by ten. In the middle of the floor was a full-size bed, one dresser with a mirror on the opposite wall, a nightstand and a small propane heater. Once little Ron had his night clothes on, given warm milk, he went to sleep from exhaustion.

My husband and I were alone. He tried to avoid me and all the questions that I demanded answers to. We argued just about all night until I had only a whimper of a voice. At that moment, I felt as if I hated him. I shipped household goods, as well as, extra money so when we arrived, foundational necessities would already be in place. He had spent the money and the household goods where in storage on his base.

*Surely, this could not be love. Was I having a bad dream? If so, I needed to wake up!*

For months, I had envisioned a smooth, happy transition. I hoped that he would make sure that all things were in place as he welcomed us into our new life.

*Not so!*

At this point, I wanted to go back home. I felt like I had been used for personal gain. In later days to come, I did find out that when your family is with you, the wife no longer receives an allotment check. Her portion is added to the soldier's base pay, with extra financial allocations for living off Post.

We didn't even have our own transportation.

*How could I have made such a grave mistake?* I asked myself repeatedly.

Because of limited bed space, my husband made his bed on the floor. My skin breakout was getting worse by the day. I had filled prescriptions of Cortisone before I left Pittsburgh, but now I was running low.

*Marie Jenkins', My Time*

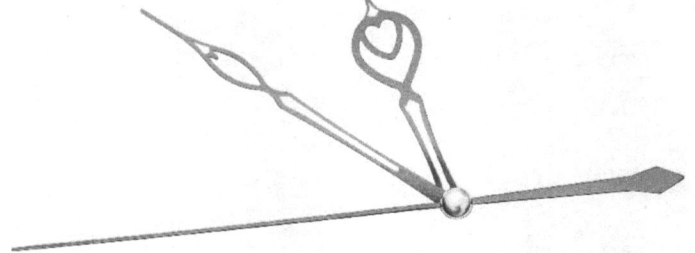

# Chapter Twelve: Lost in Sorrow

*Cold, Challenges, and Concerns*

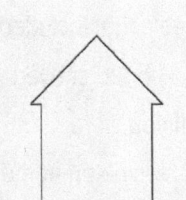

*I had made a huge mistake that involved my life and that of another – my son. In my mind, there was no way to reconcile this situation that could be considered decent, rational, or explained with integrity.*

Morning came and at five o'clock a.m. the men left for the army base. Once little Ron and I prepared ourselves for the day, we joined Nancy and Billy for breakfast. It was very difficult adjusting our taste buds to their cuisine. I had juice and coffee. Little Ron did manage to enjoy a bowl of oatmeal, a slice of toast, and a small glass of juice. As the babies played, I assisted Nancy with the cleanup of breakfast dishes. This time together gave us both an opportunity to continue the introduction from last night.

We did not have a car to get around the small town, but Nancy informed me that most of the shops were within walking distance.

*It's not the walking I mind, it's the inclement, frigid temperature that concerns me.* I thought.

Prior to the trip, I learned how to convert American money to German currency and was proficient with its usage. Nancy and I bundled the children and headed out for the market. When we reached the entrance, Nancy introduced me to Mrs. Hilda and Mr. Klaus, the landlords of the building. They were an older husband and wife couple. I would guess their ages to be in their late fifties. They both smiled and welcomed me. They owned the bar/grille restaurant that occupied much of the first floor. I discovered the two served lunch and dinner meals that included, wiener-schnitzel (breaded veal cutlets) and bratwurst with red shaved cooked cabbage. Both entrées came with dark beer. If you were ordering for children, soft drinks were available. I was fascinated at the edifice. The workers were dressed in their native apparel right down to their clogs.

Once outside, I had to carry little Ron because the snow was too deep for him to walk through. It was so cold. You could hear the howling whistle of the bitter wind ravish your body. It took control! One's defense from this wind monster was in layering clothing. As we walked down the hill, tears began rolling down my checks expressing the inter distress of my body. I held Ron close to my bosom, shielding him from the piercing edge of the wind.

After stopping at the bank to exchange money, we continued to the shops. We stopped in each the gifts shops to get warm. Finally, we reached the food vendors. There were a couple of items I purchased. Since I was not aware of our tenure as house guest, therefore, I limited the grocery list to accommodate our eating habits: baby food, breakfast foods, fruits, vegetables, chicken, wieners, ground meat. The most excruciating part of the experience was climbing the hill back to the apartment. Between the elevation and the wind in your back, it was enough to take your breath away. When we arrived, I gave the Lord a prayer of thanksgiving.

Soon the men were home. Dinner was simple, hot dogs, french fries, and pork n beans. Nothing that appeased to my appetite. I did not display or engage in a jovial reception. I remained solemn throughout dinner and the evening. I needed personal time to confer with my husband. There were unanswered questions mounting in my head. There was nowhere to go but to the confinement of the bedroom, which was comparable to a jail cell. The harder I pressed for answers with truth, the more I was convinced he was a liar, selfish, unapologetic, and not ready for the responsibility of a wife and son. I was devastated!

I had made a huge mistake that involved my life and that of another – my son. In my mind, there was no way to reconcile this situation that could be considered decent, rational or explained with integrity. He claimed we were on the list for an apartment, but no time frame was given when our apartment would become available. Nor had he communicated with the landlords regarding my concerns. I was existing on the cusp of a life altering situation. I felt like I was at the gate of hell. And those who were residents were eager for my arrival.

I discovered that I do not like Nancy. She displayed independence in having things her way. I did not like her big fat husband, the Sergeant. He was demanding, overbearing, fat (it bears repeating) and ugly. I did not like their son, little Billy. He was a bully! Consequently, I would be teaching little Ron how to defend himself. Similarly, I did not like my husband!

Mornings had challenges. I was flustered, out of character, and always had a headache! I would not engage in conversation with Nancy. I made a covenant with myself, that if Billy pushed little Ron one more time, and his mother did nothing, it might be the last time he would be able to sit down, comfortably.

Living in their apartment (the witch of the east, her water head looking son and obese, ratchet husband) was like living in a hell hole. One month and ten days passed before we signed the lease to our apartment located on the third floor, just opposite of theirs on the second floor.

With the impending move, I had jovial expectations – thoughts of realizing freedom just outside my grasp. While turning the key I envisioned this would be our castle. However, when I opened the door, I was so disappointed.

The vision I had of grandeur dissipated in one glance. I was shocked beyond belief! The entrance hall of the apartment looked like a dungeon. It reeked with musk and old smells. The hallway was like a tunnel that seemed to go on forever. However, peeking through the darkness of the hall at the far end was a light protruding in the distance. I was fearful to allow little Ron to leave my arms. I turned around to the outside hall where the luggage sat. With my right leg, I kicked all three pieces of our luggage pass the door sill, into the hall. I then closed the door and locked it behind me. With the door shut the lighting was not as vibrant. With limited visibility, my hand searched for a light switch. After locating it, I immediately turned on the hall light which revealed even more of our unfavorable situation.

The bulb wattage illuminating from the round flush ceiling mount was disappointing and produced a dim glow that was aggravating at best. (Someone was obviously trying to save money). With Ron on my hip, together we explored our new surroundings. To my immediate left was a vaulted ceiling that gave way to a nook where boots, hats and coats could be hung. Moving forward down the hall, on the right side, was a room that only had a toilet. Beside it was a bidet. The walls were shaded with taupe and brown and the same light fixture was attached to the ceiling as the hallway. The door to the small room was extremely thick and heavy, even to close. Each carved wood panel had an ornate design. And a brass doorknob was located on the left side of the door. All the doors turned out to be the same.

The next room was larger than the previous. The contents of this room housed a white tub held by four porcelain lions' feet, and a white toilet. Above the toilet was a wooden box attached to the wall. Underneath the wooden box was a hanging chain. And when pulled it flushed the toilet.

To the right of the toilet was a white bidet. Across from the tub sat an old linen closet. Accessed by two wooden doors, attached with two brass handles. The same style lighting and wall colors were repeated.

The further we walked into the belly of the dungeon; I could trace my footsteps in the dust from the floor. The next room was a larger bedroom. The walls were covered with an unappealing dingey floral pattern of taupe and green as a background. The wallpaper covered the entire room. There were no windows in any of the rooms down the hall. In the middle of the bedroom was a full-size wooden bed frame, one flat pillow, draped with a dusty green duvet. On the opposite wall was a wooden salon era ladies' dresser complete with a hand painted porcelain basin and pitcher. Mounted to the dresser was a swivel mirror stained with various thickness of dust.

Giving the illusion of odd shapes, in the adjacent corner from the dresser was an overstuff chair and ottoman. The color and design of the chair/ottoman eludes me. The next and final door displayed a smaller bedroom. It revealed a single bed, small unfinished, wood, kid size dresser. A wooden toy box was positioned at the foot of the bed. On the right side of the bed stood a miniature, wooden rocking chair. As we moved on to view the remaining rooms of the apartment, I was getting more and more traumatized.

The end of the hall ushered us into a very large room. The living room had dual usage. It served as a dining room, a well. On the left side of the room set a large wooden dining room table with four wood chairs underneath. The sofa in the living matched the same flowery print of the chair in the larger bedroom. Two square wooden tables rested on each side of the overstuffed couch. In front of the couch stood a longer version of the side tables. Two extremely tall windows faced the side of the building, only allowing a narrow view of the village. Around the corner from the living room was a small kitchen nestled in an area that seemed to be two by four. The refrigerator and the stove were apartment size. Despite the size of the stove, there were four small burners. The stove was fueled by propane gas. The can was connected on the right side. Just behind the stove stood the white refrigerator, doors rounded, freezer at the top. The sink was securely lodged under four cabinets. Across from the sink stood a four-leg medal, yellow Formica top table with two matching chairs. `

After I gained my composure from the horrifying tour, I had to figure out where to start.

At that present moment, little Ron and I were both hungry. I didn't have any food to cook. We had been munching on peanut butter crackers. I thought about the Inn down on the first floor and decided that's where little Ron and I could get lunch. I left the apartment headed for the steps. My thoughts were not comforting or pleasant.

With each step, I was reminded of the disappointment that was waiting on my return and even now (so many years later) tears stream down my face. I was lost in sorrow! I did not have a clue of an escape or how things would turn out.

Finally, we reached the Pub and were welcomed.

*Marie Jenkins', My Time*

I wasn't sure if there would be anything on the menu for little Ron, but the waitress informed me that they had mashed potatoes, gravy, and applesauce.

Perfect!

# Chapter Thirteen: Acclimating

*Coming Alive & Fighting Back*

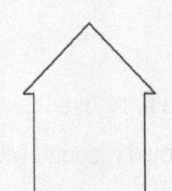

*Well, I was beside myself. I was celebrating my child's first show of self-defense. I was clapping my hands. I had rose from the couch and positioned myself in an upright posture on the floor, jumping up and down.*

As the days rolled into weeks, the apartment began to come alive and livable.

Because there were no facilities to wash and dry clothes, I purchased a scrub board, clothesline and clothespins. Twice a week, Mondays and Thursdays, were wash days. I used the bathtub as the wash machine (without a motor) and the wash board (powered by my hands) became the motor. I must confess the white clothes were like new fallen snow - white! I made use of the long hallway to string the clothesline.

Tuesdays and Wednesdays were days I designated for cleaning the apartment. After little Ron ate lunch, I would put him down for a nap. This gave me the opportunity to finish cleaning. Spring was approaching. I wanted to address areas within the apartment that were not part of my regular routine. This heavy-duty job needed extra cleaning power. So, I mix a cocktail of Spic and Span, Clorox and Mr.

Clean to the cleaning water. I decided I would start with the hallway and then proceed to the other rooms.

When I regained consciousness, little Ron was shaking me crying. I had passed out from the fumes. After that incident I *really* suffered with eczema breakout.

Corresponding with my family help me to remain content. I looked forward each week to getting a letter and pictures. I would respond with picture up-dates and verbiage.

Now that I had my own place and was settling in somewhat, Nancy and I patched up our differences. We would take the boys for walks, different outside activities and shopping throughout the village. When the husbands were not having drills on the weekend, Big Sergeant would take us for a ride in the country. The landscape was breathtaking. While the weather was still spring (summer was approaching) the four of us planned a family trip together, with the children, for a three-day weekend in Frankfurt, Germany.

I was impressed with the city of Frankfurt. It reminded me of New York City. Excitement was everywhere. We checked into a low budget hotel that I cannot recall the name. But, I certainly can remember the bathrooms located at the end of hallways. I have never seen then or now such a tightly monitored system of water usage, where you pay as you use it. The bathtub and sink faucets were affixed with metal boxes that controlled the amount of water flow. To receive water, Deutsche marks had to be inserted into the coin slot, which dispensed a measured amount of water. It was quite an experience getting enough water to bathe, wash hands or even brush your teeth. Under these conditions, the apartment did not seem so distasteful. Driving back to Wildflicken, I listened to the conversations of others. I was silent, pondering the events of the trip.

The summer months moved seamlessly. In the same context as yesterday, fall was upon us, settling into the landscape of nature. The tree leaves were turning beautiful, vibrant colors. From a panoramic view they formed a collage of yellow, orange and brown. The fall months breezed swiftly by and soon the snow was falling, and the village was beginning to decorate for the season of Christmas.

As the days and weeks approached the celebrated event, carolers in the evening would sing in front of the Pub, in German and in English. I noticed most of the villagers would give the kids holidays treats. Having treats for the carolers was out of my normal grocery shopping experience.

By the way, did I share with you my grocery shopping experience? Indeed, you will be surprised how two people who do not speak each other's language can communicate and complete a transaction!

A few blocks from the apartment was a grocery store where the proprietor only spoke German. We developed a unique method of communication for buying and selling. Vegetables, fruit and breads were open in straw baskets. I would choose the items needed, such as: potatoes, onions, tomatoes, lettuce, red cabbage, yams. If I had a question regarding the safety of unfamiliar foods, I would hold the item up, point to Ron, point to his mouth, while nodding my head yes or no. She would respond with a gesture of nay or yea. But paying for groceries took on a whole new dimension of non-verbal eye and hand signals. The proprietor would manually add the grocery items. Once a total was established, she would indicate to me by looking up that it was time to pay. I would hold up one Deutschemark next to one finger. In turn, she would hold up fingers indicating the number of Deutschemark needed to complete the transaction. If smaller denominations were needed, they were placed in the palm of my hand where she could remove what was needed.

We had a special relationship. I became very fond of her. She stood only five feet one inch. She always wore a babushka and dresses with multiple lawyering. I suspected that the one-inch heel, front tie lace-up black ankle boots increased her statue.

In two weeks, Old St. Nicholas would visit the village of Wildflecken. My Christmas shopping was completed. Sgt. Jim took his wife and me to the Post Exchange (PX) located on the army post. The PX was a store much like Wal Mart and there I was able to get the Christmas presents I needed. We purchased a small Charlie Brown Christmas tree. Decorations were scarce, just a few colorful bulbs with a single string of lights, due to the lack of funds. Squeezing the budget, I managed to purchase an angel for the top of the tree.

Christmas morning came with excitement when little Ron laid his eyes on the three-piece rideable train. It had an engine with a horn that would whistle when pulled, a middle flat car, which had a storage area where he could put his other toys, and a caboose. It was later in the afternoon when little Ron discovered there were additional toys under the tree from Santa. They were one small wooden puzzle, a bag of army soldiers, a small car and a coloring book with crayons. I extended an invitation to Nancy and Billy to spend a couple hours so that the boys could play together. Big Ron was invited by his Sergeant to watch a football game, in his apartment, while the boys played.

At first, Billy and little Ron greeted each other with sharing the toys they each received. Little Ron climbed on the train to show Billy what it would do. After several laps around the living room, Billy became impatient waiting for his turn and suddenly pushed little Ron off the train and made him cry. Once again, I looked to Nancy for correction. As all ways, there was no reaction or correction. Billy was taller and heavier than little Ron. Which always gave him the advantage. He was mean and selfish. Now, Billy was mounting himself upon the engine. But this time little Ron emerged from a fallen position and decided to fight back. He hit him right in the "kisser" which knocked him off the train.

Well, I was beside myself. I was celebrating my child's first show of self-defense. I was clapping my hands. I had rose from the couch and positioned myself in an upright posture on the floor, jumping up and down.

Billy ran to his mother crying. Nancy decided to take Billy home. She gathered his toys, picked Billy up and headed for the door. I didn't even hear her say good-bye. I was rejoicing as I comforted little Ron on his bravery.

I remembered all the times Billy bullied little Ron and Nancy never corrected his aggressive behavior.

# Chapter Fourteen: Returning to the States

*Regrets and Shock*

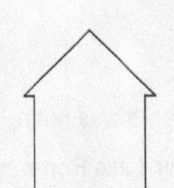

*Once in the bathroom I began to peel down the layers of clothing that restricted me. In horror, I discovered I was standing in a pool of blood. I was hemorrhaging profusely. I was going into shock!*

The month of January presented challenging obstacles. As I packed to return home to the state of Pittsburgh, the weather was brutally inclement. Little did I know, my husband's platoon was scheduled for war games. This activity required two weeks in quarantine. The second and third week of January were designated for the exercise and for me were unbearably lonely and fearful. I continued each day to pack a box. Some days I just cried.

The apartment's insulation no longer kept the outside howling wind at bay. In every room of the house, I felt wind drafts. I was concerned for the well-being of both little Ron and I, not wanting us to catch colds, nor the flu. Throughout the day, when the rooms were not producing enough heat to keep us warm, I would light the oven in the kitchen, open the door and position a chair in between the kitchen and the living room, so we both could absorb heat. I felt we were prisoners in a strange country in that apartment, confined to one area of comfort.

The first week of confinement left scars on my body. My skin was not only dryer than usual, but scratching was a torment. I realize now (and even then) that it was prayer that brought us through:

*"Yea though I walk through the valley of the shadow of death..."*
**Psalm 23:4.**

The following Sunday afternoon, I was preparing dinner. It was not a typical southern meal, just hamburgers and french fries. Little Ron was easy to please. Halfway through the cooking process of the burgers, the right front burner and pilot went out! I didn't know what to do. I was frantic as tears began to form, I started shaking the stove back and forth. When that action did not produce a response, I kicked it. I was so overcome with frustration until I began to regret my previous decision to join my husband in Germany. It had been one disappointment after the other.

*Why didn't he check everything before he left?* I thought on the verge of defeat.

While I sat, rocking back and forth, I began to settle down. I began to think a little clearer. The Lord had mercy on me. In a small still voice, He said, "Check the propane tank."

When I complied, the tank was empty.

I thought, "What do I do now?"

I put a jacket on little Ron, went downstairs to the Pub hoping to speak with the landlord. I explained to her what happened. I hoped that she would help me solve the dilemma. To my surprise, I could not believe her response.

"The propane tank needs to be refilled," she said with a roll of her eyes.

"How can I refill it?" I pressed.

"In the village," she said in hasty tone. Then sensing my bewilderment, "If you don't have the finance to pay, you can charge it through your husband's Commanding Officer."

"How do I get to the village store?"

She responded with the same sarcasm in her voice, "If you do not have a vehicle, you walk."

I was so out done. I felt like someone had captured my being and doused me in cold water. I was fighting back tears as I thanked her and returned to the apartment.

*What am I going to do?* I kept asking myself.

I was in a dilemma. I started calling on the Lord and my mother for help. I whispered a prayer, dried my tears, put my pride in the closet, went to the second-floor apartment, knocked on the door, and prayed that Nancy would greet me with a warm embrace.

After, I announced who I was, she opened the door with a bewildered look. I stood in my position as I humbly revealed the circumstance which I was facing. Surprisingly, she welcomed both little Ron and I to join her in the living room. Before I could murmur another word, Nancy reached for little Ron, expressed to me that she would keep him until I got back. I was stunned and relieved at the same time. I thanked her, spoke to Billy, and kissed little Ron as I made my way to the door. (The previous prayer included my concern for little Ron having interaction with Billy.) I believed the Lord would watch over him as I left him with Nancy and Billy. I needed to handle the situation at hand.

I disconnected the tank. It was not heavy or awkward. The store was down the hill from the apartment building. I tried to humor the occasion. I would roll the tank and catch up with it until I reached the bottom of the hill. Turning left at the corner, I saw the store! The proprietors were gracious. They spoke English! The wait was not long before the tank was filled. I did not have enough money, so the balance was charged to my husband. When I tried to pick the tank up, I could not. The tank was too heavy for me to carry. Again, tears began to well up in my eyes. I had come this far.

One of the owners tied a rope made of jute around the top of the tank. Perhaps, I could pull it up the hill. I was struggling to get the tank out of the store onto flat ground. I looked for anyone who could help me. I pulled the tank to the bottom of the hill.

*I can do this,* I said to myself.

I dug my boots in the hard snow pulling the tank behind me. Halfway to the top I turned around and pulled the tank walking backwards. Changing positions back and forth slowly up the hill felt like I was moving in slow motion gaining two steps and losing one. I began to not only get tired, but every bone in my body was sore. My shoulders were stretched to capacity. I stopped to rest several times.

Moving forward, I felt warmth running down my leg. I ignored the intrusion. I had to complete the assignment.

Finally, after what seemed like forever, I reached the apartment building. None of the German men from the Pub who saw me as they were leaving, offered their assistance. I sat on the step for a while to gain composure. One step at a time, I pulled the propane can up two flights of steps until I reached the apartment. Opening the door, I then rolled the can to the end of the hallway. I continued the practice until I reached the stove and hooked it up.

Then I laid in the floor and thanked God:

"Thank you, Lord for your grace and mercy. Thank you for giving me strength."

I regained my composure and reunited with Nancy and the boys. To my surprise, Billy and little Ron were playing nice together. Prayer does work!

Once little Ron and I settled back into the apartment. I had an urgency to use the bathroom. Before I went out into the cold to have the propane can filled, I donned myself with layers of clothing. I put on one pair of thick leggings under waterproof sweatpants. The bottom of the pants was tucked inside two wool cable socks, and firmly secure by rugged soul boots. My upper torso was also layered with several heavy sweaters. I wore a winter scarf around my neck. My head was covered first by a babushka, skull cap and finally a hood. My coat was long enough to reach my knees. The draw string at the end of the coat, when pulled keep me warm.

Once in the bathroom I began to peel down the layers of clothing that restricted me. In horror, I discovered I was standing in a pool of blood. I was hemorrhaging profusely. I was going into shock! I had to pull myself together enough to remember how this occurred. Reflecting on the events of the day, it must have occurred during the steepest part of the hill. When I continued pulling, I felt something pop inside of my lower extremities. I did not address the matter at that time. I was engaged with one thought, getting the propane can connected to the stove. I was frantic. My husband was not scheduled to return from the field for another two and a half weeks.

After my husband returned from the field, he was exhausted and detached from the realities of home life. When I shared with him my physical condition due to struggling with the propane gas can, he suggested I continue home treatments. He expressed, "you seem to be getting stronger each day. Whatever you are doing is working." He reminded me of our lack of transportation needed to get to the Infirmity of the Military Base.

I finished packing. In two days, little Ron and I would be on a flight back home. I was delighted to leave. The experiences I had in Germany would live in the archives of my memories for a lifetime.

Before our departure, I thanked Nancy for sharing her accommodations and kindness with us. I kissed Billy on the cheek. Once downstairs, I said good-bye to the landlord before we left for the airport. I also thanked Sergeant Jim for his extended courtesy. My husband, little Ron and I exchanged salutations.

Due to the intensity of going through customs and locating our gate my heart began to have strong, erratic palpitations. It was an uncanny human experience that I have no desire to repeat. For example: the flight schedule boards were in large German print, whereas the English print was smaller and confusing when the flight(s) up-dated using cards that flipped and sounded like dominos. Once the plane peeked over the clouds my anxiety lessened.

It was time to line up for boarding. We had the same window, center and empty isle seat, as our previous flight. Except for meals, little Ron and I slept. I noticed my skin sensations were quieter. I was still hemorrhaging, but to a lesser degree.

A friendly voice came over the speaker:

"All passengers please return to your seats, put them in an up-right position and fasten your seat belts."

The plane was landing! Thank God!

## Chapter Fifteen: An Ending

*Hurt Feelings*

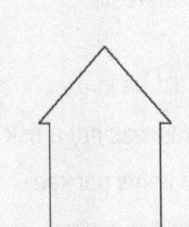

*He was cognizant in his response to my question and answered with attitude. "I could have stayed in Texas with my woman," he said with attitude in his words and body language. "You should be grateful I even made the effort to come back."*

From the airport, the Greyhound bus was our connecting transportation to Pittsburgh. Pulling into the bus station in Pittsburgh, I could see my mother and God mother waiting for us. A big smile filled my face. I was happy to see them. I took little Ron's hand and began to wave to them through the bus window. I was excited to be home!

Stepping off the bus, with open arms, we were welcomed by Mom and DeeDee with hugs and kisses. On our drive to the house, I shared several memories of Germany. They asked many questions. Some I could answer and some (for example regarding the culture of other surrounding countries, such as Denmark) I could not because I hadn't visited those places. We laughed as they shared their stories with me regarding the family and church.

*I'm back.* I said to myself. The moment felt like old time fellowship.

Little Ron and I stayed on the third floor of my parent's house until I was able to secure housing. Big Ron received orders, while in Germany, that reassigned his tour to Texas. He requested that we join him. This time he had rank, which enabled him to receive housing on Post. However, due to my previous experience in Germany, I was not interested!

I wanted to make sure little Ron and I's next home would be in a reliable, safe environment. Joining my husband in Texas was not a risk I was willing to engage. (I never received the household items packed from Germany.) I immersed myself into being a responsible, loving mother. I was able to enrolled in a two-year Business School. A year later during the Christmas holidays, Big Ron came home to spend the Christmas season with us and our families (so I thought).

It was the week of Christmas, in fact, on Christmas eve, my husband's brothers invited him to join them for drinks, catching up and reconnecting with old friends. Apparently, we were not top priority. Big Ron returned home at 3:30 a.m., drunk, staggering, talking crazy, eyes glazed over, with a stench of foreign substances. I was furious! He was laughing, reliving his night of wild parting of ill repute. I was broken. How could I possibly think our relationship would improve? Especially taking into account past experiences. I always believed he did not want to be a responsible husband or father based upon his actions. But I still had faith or hope that just maybe…

Perhaps, I was holding on to hopeful desires long buried with disappointments. Even in his current state of intoxication, I confronted him.

"Why would spend more time with your brothers and friends than with us? You haven't been home in almost a year." I stated the obvious. "And we might not see you for another year."

He was cognizant in his response to my question and answered with attitude. "I could have stayed in Texas with my woman," he said with attitude in his words and body language. "You should be grateful I even made the effort to come back."

Well, his answer changed the protectory of us going forward. I visioned a new future without him! I was in complete attack mode! Then with all the fervor I could muster fire in my bosom, hands on my hips, head positioned to the side I prepared to give him a full throttle response.

"Upon your departure and before you return, I will no longer be your wife!"

He nodded his response in a nonchalant manner as he made his bed on the living room floor.

He left after New Year's which gave me time to secure a Divorce Attorney. Upon the advice of my attorney, he strongly suggested for me to restore my maiden name. Approximately, nine months later, I received a phone call from my attorney. The divorce papers were served, signed, and waiting to be pick up. The call was bittersweet. It felt like a dagger had been plunged into my heart. Little Ron would be affected by his mother's decision and his father's mistakes. I felt like a failure! The church would assign the scarlet letter to my life. I would be shunned by some, ostracized by others. I feared that little Ron may not have the joy of father son activities together. I felt I had fallen down, losing the two steps I had gained.

What I thought was a consensual dissolution of marriage became a nightmare. Ron returned home and began to continually stalk me morning and night. He knew where I was employed. When I left for work, he would be standing close enough to attract my attention. As if to say, "I'm watching you." These actions took a toll on my mind and condition of my skin.

I filed for child support through Juvenile Court. Ron would not contribute financial support to little Ron, nor make any arrangements with me to do so. I informed Juvenile Court of his non-payments. He was served a court summon to appear before the judge. I sat on the opposite side of the table while he defended his inability to make payments. All I was hearing were lies, lies, lies. What he was saying was all lies. While pushing back tears, I could not comprehend why someone (the father) had to be forced to take care a child that belonged to them! I continued to express hurt feelings. I could no longer hold back my tears! As they streamed down my checks, rolling underneath my chin, I addressed the court with my final appeal.

"I will take care *my* son without his financial help!"

I left the court room, broken, embarrassed, feeling helpless. Months later (October of 1982) I received a letter from Juvenile Court, informing me that little Ron was awarded seventy-eight dollars every two weeks for child support and the date of dispersal.

I had not received a check.

Disgusted, I tore up the letter, discarding it in the trash can.

*Marie Jenkins', My Time*

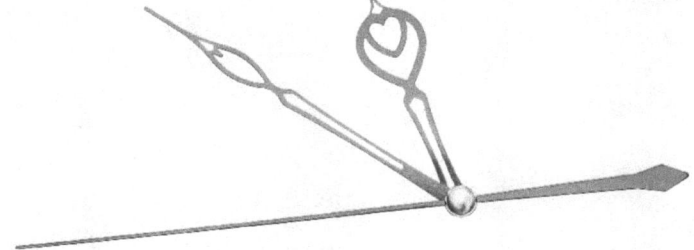

# Chapter Sixteen: Vengeance

*A Cry for Help*

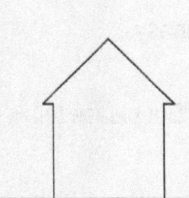

*"We received a phone call from a woman. The voice sounded like yours. She was screaming that her life was in danger. She said someone was beating her and pleaded out in agony for us to come get her," he said.*

Early one morning around 2:30 a.m., I was awakened out of a deep sleep by the pounding on the sliding glass door, downstairs. I was disorientated. I pulled myself together to confront the situation. With fear and a hammer in my right hand, I slowly moved towards the disruptive sounds.

Once downstairs, I saw a figure liken unto a man. As I got closer the gleam of the streetlight provided a reflection from the newly fallen snow enough to recognize that it was indeed a man!

Just as I was ready to dial 911, a voice spoke to me from the other side of the glass. I recognized the voice to be my father. I invited him in from the cold to join me. He was shivering and sweating profusely. Dad had a look of fear in his eyes, that I had only witnessed once before, when he thought I was lost. His breathing was labored and shallow. I was concerned for his heart.

*Why was he here? What could be the nature of this visit?*

I lived approximately thirty miles from where my parents resided. I was so confused! My father had questions too.

"Are you alright? Is everything ok?"

I had been, but his questions were making me very uneasy.

"Dad, I'm fine," I said, doing my best to reassure him. "But please tell me what is wrong."

Finally, he explained the reason for his trip.

"We received a phone call from a woman. The voice sounded like yours. She was screaming that her life was in danger. She said someone was beating her and pleaded out in agony for us to come get her," he said. I could hear the panic still fresh in his voice even now knowing that I was ok.

So, my dad immediately decided to drive thirty miles, in snow and ice to rescue me.

"Is little Ron ok," my dad asked.

"Yes," I said. Thankfully, he had not been disturbed by any of the commotion.

Dad and I sat together at the table with a cup of hot chocolate regaining our composure. It had been a daunting experience. When day light appeared, Dad calmly gave me a hug. I asked him to call when he got home. Feeling relieved, he made the journey back home. I had not experienced a breakout in a while, but that night's trauma ignited the itch. My mind continued reliving the incident over and over.

I was hurt for the pain this caused my parents. I was grateful to God how He watched over my father making the trip. And I was angry! I wanted to know who this woman was impersonating me.

*Who would cause this horrible pain on my parents?*

It was a few weeks later before we found out. It was my ex-husband. By his own admission he was trying to use scare tactics to get me back. He was determined I would always be his wife!

I decided not to press charges against little Ron's father for the turmoil and anguish he caused us. Instead, my eldest brother confronted him one evening which convinced him not to continue with his madness. Several years later my ex-husband transitioned from this life due to lung cancer.

As Ronnie grew in height and statue, he wanted to be addressed as "Ron." He no longer wanted to be called little Ron.

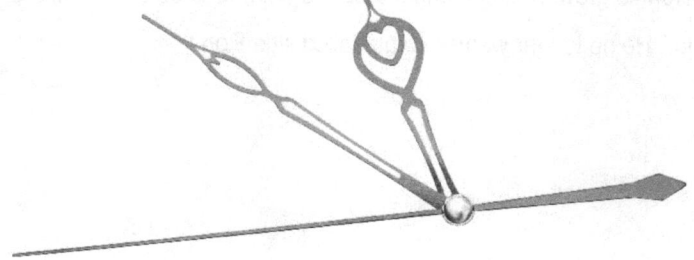

# Chapter Seventeen: Enjoying Life

*A Night with Diana*

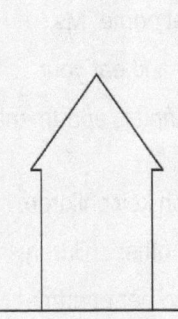

As the fall weeks rolled into summer months the Diana Ross revue was coming to Pittsburgh for a one-night performance. I desired to go. I asked my manager if I could leave two hours earlier that day. After checking to see if anyone else was out on leave, he granted my request. Excited beyond measure, not only did I purchase my ticket, I treated myself to a new outfit.

Ron and I were financially struggling. I was seeking a better paying job. At the time, I was working for a local bank as a teller. The daily travel was cumbersome. I took two buses going to work and two buses back from work. Because of the distance in which I had to travel; Ron became a latch key child. Each morning before I left for work, we would eat breakfast together and talk. I always reminded him to call me when he got home, first, before anything else. When the weather was inclement, getting home from work at my normal time was always delayed. This further increased my stress level.

Ron and I were new tenets in our apartment building. One summer evening my neighbor introduced herself to me. We sat on my patio and talked for hours. Ron ran in and out of the apartment for water and bathroom breaks. On one such occasion I introduced him to her.

"Ron, this is Ms. Annie," I began. "She has agreed to watch out for you when you come home each day after school. The same routine we have now will still apply. You must call me when you first get home. Ms. Annie and I have agreed after you change your cloths and eat your snack, you can take your homework with you to Ms. Annie's apartment."

Ron was thrilled. Ms. Annie watched several other latch key children. She felt Ron would be welcomed and interact with the other children. Ron thanked me and Ms. Annie. She invited me over to her apartment to see all the board and electronic games, puzzles, and toys. She also had outside sport activities: football, basketball, regular balls, volleyball and bat mitten. There was also skates, hula hoops, jacks, jump ropes and sidewalk chalk. I was impressed and so thankful for her warm hospitality.

"I provide snacks for all the children too," Ms. Annie informed me. "Ron is welcome to eat with them."

Ms. Annie never discussed a fee. And when I would bring the subject to her attention, she would always say, "Do the best you can. This is my ministry."

Every two-week payday after I accounted for my tithes, I gave a reasonable portion to her. Some weeks she would accept the money, other weeks she would say, "Buy something nice for my boy, Ron."

When we could not celebrate holidays with my family due to inclement weather, we would celebrate them with Ms. Annie and her family. She was "family" to us. Eventually, she met my mother, father, and brothers. My mother and Ms. Annie became instant friends. They both were avid talkers. My father invited her to church, for Sunday morning fellowship. Ms. Annie did accept the invitation especially at Easter and Christmas.

When my father and mother became stricken with sickness and hospitalized, Ms. Annie would visit them. She would take them fruit, sing church songs, and read the Bible to my father. During the time Ron spent with Ms. Annie's, they formed a special bond of love. The bond between them existed into Ron's adult life, until she passed.

I also, loved her. I have rich, wonderful memories of our time together. She was a special friend sent to us by God. Knowing that Ron would be secure, I took a sigh of relief! My stress level decreased, and I didn't have as many skin breakouts.

I submitted several applications to banks looking for a Control Teller. However, the interviews were not in my favor. I was rejected several times either because of the lack of experience or I was not a good fit for the organization. I had three-year experience as a teller. The Control Teller where I was employed started training me how to do her job. I was appreciative of the confidence she had in me, however, there was not an opening. The bank only had one branch. Unless she was ready to retire or they created another position, there was no opportunity for advancement. I continued to submit applications as I went to work each day.

One afternoon while at work I received a phone call during my lunch hour from the Human Resources Department at a competitor bank. They were requesting an interview and wanted to know if I was interested.

"Yes," I responded emphatically.

This bank had become one of the largest banks in Pittsburgh. The morning of the interview I prayed that God would grant me favor. The interview was held in their corporate building. Upon arrival I was greeted by the Human Resource Department Secretary.

"Welcome," she greeted me. "You may have a seat, and someone will be with you shortly. I'll let them know that you are here. Help yourself to the complimentary breakfast bar while you wait."

"Thank you," I offered, but I was too nervous to eat or drink.

Just I was getting comfortable in the soft leather chair, my name was called. A short man with a bushy beard, round frame glasses, gorgeous thick black curly hair and a million-dollar smile, invited me into his office. Mr. Radcliff allowed me to get comfortable. In my heart I had an assurance concerning the job. It would be offered to me. And it was!

I had a full time Control Teller position. I was so excited! I was having joyful heart palpitations. I thanked the Lord over and over. I couldn't wait to share the good news with Ron, my parents and Ms. Annie. When I shared my good news, everyone was so happy for me. Ron grabbed me around the waist with glee. My mother had prayed, and the Lord responded with allowing me to get the position.

Ms. Annie not only gave me congratulatory comments, but she also invited Ron and I for dinner. We dined sufficiently on collard greens, macaroni and cheese, southern fried chicken, homemade corn bread and lemonade. I was so full of the main course, I didn't have enough room for pound cake. I would take it for my lunch the next day.

Felling stuffed and sleepy, I made my way back to my apartment. Once I located the bed, it began to call me. Ron reluctantly followed me. He wanted to stay up, but it was a school night and a workday in the morning for me.

At my new job, I only had to catch one bus to work. I was in the heart of downtown Pittsburgh. I had accessibility. I could walk a couple of blocks to the job from the bus drop-off. I introduced myself to staff and was greeted with a warm reception. They had cake in the lunchroom with "Welcome Marie." I really felt special. Most of my first day was getting acquainted with their operational system.

The first day was challenging to say the least. Not only did I control the uninterrupted performance of the teller line, I prepared financial shipment for the Brink truck. Food stamps had to be balanced against invoices and reported to the State of Pittsburgh and teller cash flow was constantly being replenished. And to add insult to injury, quite often I was summoned to resolve disputes between the customer and a teller.

After the bank was closed, the teller line could not leave until the bank was balanced. There were evenings when trying to find the mistake was grueling. Yet, I did not complain. Financially, I was able with comfort and cushion (having a bank saving account), to take care of Ron and myself.

As the fall weeks rolled into summer months the Diana Ross revue was coming to Pittsburgh for a one-night performance. I desired to go. I asked my manager if I could leave two hours earlier that day. After checking to see if anyone else was out on leave, he granted my request. Excited beyond measure, not only did I purchase my ticket, I treated myself to a new outfit. I had previously asked Ms. Annie if Ron could stay a few hours longer? She said it would be no problem.

Finally, it was Friday, the day of the Diana Ross event. I arrived at work that morning informing the teller line of my early plans to leave. Therefore, all end of the day request for startup drawer money for Monday morning would need to be turned in by 12:00 noon. All the tellers complied. I called each teller into the vault to verify the amount requested was given. Then both myself and the teller initialed the voucher for authenticity. Voucher totals were added to the money of account in the vault, verified and signed by the Control Teller and

Branch Manager. Once the vault currency was balanced, I continued to carry out the rest of my functions for the day. Watching the clock from time to time, two o'clock would be reached in ten minutes. For the last time I conferred with the Branch Manager regarding closing. I began to gather my belongings. At two o'clock on the dot, I wished everyone a wonderful weekend and left the bank to meet my girlfriend.

We met under the historic clock at Macys. The concert doors would open in a few hours. So, we had time to get a hamburger, fries, and drink. When we finished eating, we started walking towards the event center. The line had already begun to form. We joined the end of the line, hoping the doors would open soon. Once we were in the building, we went to the lady's room and changed into our concert evening cloths. I wore a one-piece black cat-suit. You could not tell me I wasn't the bell of the ball. All I needed were the glass slippers.

My friend (Debbie) wore a two-piece rhinestone top and form fitting bell bottoms. She out shined me with stones, but she could not touch me with the sassiness of how the cat-suit lined my figure. The lights in the hall were flashing. The show was about to start.

We had good seating in the middle section about ten rows from the stage. The house lights darkened the auditorium, and a baritone voice filled the room with housekeeping instructions. Everyone was chanting Diana's name. Finally, the voice demanded silence as the formal introduction unfolded:

"Ladies and gentlemen, Pittsburgh is bringing to the stage, the one, the only, like none other, Ms. Diana Ross!"

The people's voices erupted in intensified feelings of expression. The house was cheering as Ms. Ross ran down the middle isle dragging a red boa draped over one shoulder saying, "I've come a long way."

As she took the stage, she belted out in a soft soprano voice singing *Endless Love*. She was joined on the stage by Luther Vandross making one of his many debuts. By this time, I was mesmerized. The concert was amazing. Ms. Ross ended the evening of splendor with *Reach Out and Touch Somebody's Hand*. I was spellbound by the grandiosity of it all.

Debbie had a car. We drove home chatting and reliving the evening. It was late when I checked in with Ms. Annie and asked her to send Ron home.

"He's sleep and resting well," she told me. "I'll send him home in the morning."

I thanked her and said good night. It was difficult getting to sleep that night. I was so overwhelmed by the experience I encountered earlier.

Sure, enough Ron returned home the next morning to kiss me, get cereal, take a shower, change clothes, and meet with the kids outside for a game of morning baseball. Some of the little boys were knocking loudly on the sliding glass window.

*Marie Jenkins', My Time*

Irritated I open the door and asked, "Can I help you?"

In concert they replied, 'Are you coming out to play baseball with us?"

Smiling, I replied, "Give me a moment."

As I was getting dress for the game, Ron returned with an attitude and asked, "Why are you playing? Why can't you be like other mothers?"

Instead of being upset, I answered, "Because the other mothers can't play baseball. All they do is sit around and gossip. Your team can't beat ours! Let's go."

Dressed for the occasion polyester blue shorts, an oversized white t-shirt, bobby socks with two red rings around the top and old beat-up tennis shoes, I was quickly out the door, and cheering on my team. As usual, our team won!

Ron was not in a pleasant mood when the game was over. He declared, "You all cheated!"

I responded, "My team is better, you just lost!"

Not only did the neighborhood kids play baseball, but Anne also brought a bad mitten set for us. The spring, summer and fall months were seasons filled with fun, laughter, wins and losses. During the summer months, Anne provided inflatable kid swimming pools, packed with pool toys. After the first snow fall, Ron, myself, and the kids would walk to the neighborhood grocery store and ask the manager for boxes, preferably large, that would otherwise be put in the dumpster. With a smile, the manager would comply. Each one of us was able to get one.

With big smiles and a loud grateful thank you, we returned to prepare for the sled ride. I would cut the seams of the boxes and Annie would place the boxes in large garbage bags. This would keep the box dry and protected. The front bag opening back which would serve as a hand for our home-made sleigh. It would enhance high-speed going down the hill. We had so much fun! Most of the mothers could not afford the wooden sleds with steel blades. But we didn't miss a beat! After several hours of sled riding, we stacked up our boxes on the side of my patio for the next time. Then we enjoyed hot chocolate with marshmallows at Annie's house. The room was filled with shivering, excited, loud kids. They were re-hashing their blistery fun Sunday afternoon sled ride. Announcing "the party is over," was not greeted with acceptance.

I heard moans and groans. I saw little people's faces contorted in disappointment all the while asking, "Can we stay longer? Do we have to leave now?"

Both Annie and I said, "Yes, you have to go home."

*Marie Jenkins', My Time*

# Chapter Eighteen: Through the Valley

*Battling Fear*

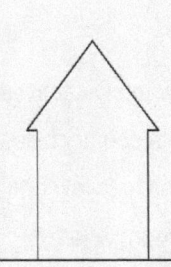

> *He cleared off the table and placed the cups and left-over donuts in the receptacle located in the corner of the room. I returned his jacket to him. I could feel my heart beating so fast! I rehearsed an inward prayer, known as the Lord's Prayer. I was getting ready to walk through the "...valley of the shadow of death." I was trying to not fear!*

The weekend always seemed to move at lighting speed compared to the work week.

Again, it was Monday morning. The routine was the same: cup of coffee for me, breakfast cereal and juice for Ron, packed lunches, moms' instructions, a prayer, then off to the challenges of the day.

When I arrived at work, the atmosphere was strained and cold with silence. There were faces that I did not recognize. When introduced, both men (African American) were City of Pittsburgh Detectives. They announced that they were waiting for the last employee to arrive. Minutes after the sentence was spoken, Nathaniel entered the room.

The shorter Detective in stature, whose last name was Lee, informed us, "The entire staff will be taken down to the precinct for finger printing." He further explained, "This is at the request of your employer."

Everyone had a puzzled look on their face, but no one asked the question, "Why?"

We were instructed to gather our belongings and follow the Detectives. Due to the inclement weather, four blocks seemed like a country mile. Once at the Police Station, our group was divided in half to follow one of the Detectives. We were ushered into a small waiting room where further instructions were given as to how the procedure would occur.

Four employees completed their test and returned to work. After some time had passed, I was ushered into a smaller room by a female officer. When I asked her questions, she was very abrasive. She finally said to me, as she was leaving the room, "Someone will be in to get you."

I began to fear! The room was small. It had one desk and two chairs. I was occupying one of chairs and began looking for a window. I gasped for air and my skin was tingling, wanting to be satisfied by scratching. Tears welled up in my eyes and streamed down my face. I had to go to the bathroom! When the female officer exited the room, I heard the door lock!

*Why was I being treated like this? Where was everyone else?*

I danced in my chair from a seated position as the pressure of relieving my bladder became urgent. Finally, I banged on the door as hard as I could. With a loud voice I demanded, "I have to go to the bathroom!"

The same stoic unpleasant female officer unlocked and opened the door motioning me to follow her. She followed me inside the women's bathroom, standing guard the door. I felt like a prisoner! By this time the morning hours had passed. It was twelve forty-five. I had not had any lunch or beverage. I felt lightheaded and sick in my stomach. As I followed the female officer back to the holding room, I did not see any of the other employees. Once the officer watched me enter the room, she slammed the door behind me and locked it, again!

I was shaking from fear of the unknown! I was still waiting when two o'clock rolled around. I was agitated and anxious. Ron would be home from school soon. And he would call me on my work phone number to let me know he was safe. I had no way to call Annie to give him a message for me. By this time, I was crying profusely. I felt like I was losing consciousness. My thoughts were all over the place.

*What would Ron do if something happened to me? He's all I have!*

My mind was giving me horrible visuals.

*What if they take me away from him?*

I was praying so hard! When I opened my eyes, everything was blurred behind my tears. I was drowning in sorrow. Finally! The door opened.

It was Detective Lee. He announced, "I will take you to the room where you will be fingerprinted."

I was so nervous, afraid, drained, worried, and hungry. I went into a breakdown. I was shivering uncontrollably, crying with deep sighs only to catch my breath and speechless to respond to his directive. Detective Lee thought I was cold. He removed his jacket and placed it around my shoulders. He was comforting me with kind words, "What's wrong? You have nothing to be afraid of."

With a warm smile he explained to me the procedure on how finger printing would be administered. I could not stop shivering or crying, I was trying very hard to articulate my feelings into words that would precipitate verbal communications. Perhaps his longevity, training and wisdom as a Detective prepared him for crisis situations such as mine. He locked his eyes with mine and asked, "Do you understood what I am saying?"

I responded with a head nod indicating, yes. Detective Lee let me know, that he would step out of the room for a moment, so I could compose myself. When he returned, he had coffee and donuts. He sat across the table from me. He smiled and said, "You choose what donut you want."

Then he slid the black coffee, stirrer, cream, and sugar to me. My hands were shaking. He helped me put the sugar and cream in my cup. I silently said a short prayer, then I took a white powered cake donut to my lips. As I continued to eat and drink, I felt my nerves settling. Just as I was finishing the donut and coffee, Detective Lee asked if I felt better.

I responded with a verbal, "Yes," followed by a consenting head nod.

He cleared off the table and placed the cups and left-over donuts in the receptacle located in the corner of the room. I returned his jacket to him. I could feel my heart beating so fast! I rehearsed an inward prayer, known as the Lord's Prayer. I was getting ready to walk through the "…valley of the shadow of death." I was trying to not fear!

Detective Lee escorted me to the room where I would be fingerprinted. When we entered the room, he placed his arm around my shoulder and said, "Be honest, and tell the truth. You will pass with flying colors."

His smile was reassuring of his faith in me. He introduced me to the Test Administrator. He was tall, robust, and kind. He indicated by pointing to "the chair" in which I would spend time with him and the "machine." Once seated the Test Administrator asked me to place my forearms in alignment with the wooden arms of the chair. My wrists were strapped with leather bands and secured with buckles. Two corrugated tubes were gently attached to the upper and lower chest area, which were used to measure my breathing. Two finger cuffs were attached to my index and ring finger on each hand. The Polygraph machine was turned on by the flip of a switch. This action vibrated in my ears. The lights on the machine came on, the needles of the graph began to swing back and forth at an accelerated movement.

This heightened activity of the machine intensified my reactions of fear and nervousness. I was uncontrollably shaking to the point that the test could not be administered. My thoughts took me to a dark place, where I was fighting for my life in an electric chair. No one was there for me. No one was there to verify my innocence. The test was postponed for a future date. On my way out of the Precinct, Detective Lee (off the record) suggested that when I return that I have a lawyer accompany me for the re-scheduled Polygraph test.

# Chapter Nineteen: Flying Colors

*Innocent*

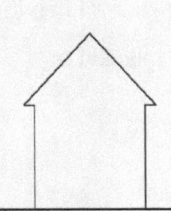

> *The allegation of charges against me were that I had not adhered to the Bank's Policy and Procedures regarding an early day approved leave. She stated that this was a breach that had consequently caused a crime to occur, embezzlement of funds.*

When I got home. I thanked Annie for watching Ron and feeding him dinner.

My head was throbbing like lightening when it cracks the sky ensued by thunder. I went to bed covering my head. I wanted to just disappear! I could not fathom what the future for Ron and I would be. I was disoriented, confused, angry, self-absorbed in pain, and wanting to end my uncertainties. My thoughts were abruptly refocused to Ron. His needs and wellbeing were dependent upon me.

*Who would care for him should something happen to me?*

My parents were well up in age. My mother could not climb steps anymore and my father had retired from his employment and was a full-time pastor and care giver to my mother. The thought of Ron's father's parents as caregivers was not an option. They did not have the means or environment to ensure his protection in successfully raising him. I was in a dilemma!

*God, please help me. Please.*

The next day wasn't any better, nor the days to follow. I knew I had to do something. So, I contacted my divorce attorney. I explained my situation and asked if he could help me.

He said, "I will look into the matter and follow up with you."

The days rolled into weeks. Ron and I were being sustained by the saving account I established. Funds were getting low with each passing week. Not only was I not being paid during the investigation and arbitration between my employer and myself, but I was also not eligible for State assistance.

Finally, my attorney got back to me after reviewing the aspects of the case.

"I will represent you," he said, "and I'll also escort you to the rescheduled Polygraph test."

The test was rescheduled for the following Monday. My attorney met me at the Precinct. Detective Lee introduced himself as the lead officer in charge of the case. My lawyer introduced himself as my counsel.

"I am here to make sure my clients rights are not violated," my attorney said firmly.

Detective Lee acknowledged his statement.

After the introductions, my name was called to be retested. I felt my frail body undergo a multitude of remembrances of the first encounter. My palms began to sweat, my mouth went dry, and my breathing was shallow. I felt very warm, disorientated, fearful of the unknown, distracted and nervous. In that moment, I recalled the pain I endured during the previous weeks that led to the importance of this day:

Not eating, allowing Ron to eat. Not sleeping in fear, I wouldn't wake up! Watching funds dwindle. Waiting for the truth to be revealed.

I closed my eyes for a moment and took a couple of deep breaths to compose my thoughts. When I opened my eyes, my attorney was standing in front of me. He placed both of his hands on my shoulders and said, "You can do this. Take your time and answer each question honestly and completely. If you feel overwhelmed, count backwards from five. I am right here on the other side of the door. I believe in you!"

With that said, I walked in the room with confidence. I had butterflies fluttering in my stomach, but this time I was not shaking.

I answered each question honestly, took my time and asked that some questions be repeated for clarity. I felt empowered! I was conquering my fears. I tried to avoid watching the graph pens in fear they would be distracting. Then I heard the Test Administrator say, 'This is the last question."

Once I answered the question, I was silently celebrating victory. The Test Administrator unbuckled me, opened the door, and announced, "Miss Marie is finished with testing."

My attorney greeted me with a warm smile of congratulations. He said, "I knew you could do it!"

"You are finished and free to go," Detective Lee informed both of us. Then he said to my attorney, "The test results will be given to Miss Marie's employer, who will pass the findings on to your client."

My attorney voiced his concerns and said, "My client and I will wait here for the results. Can you tell me Detective Lee, approximately what the wait time will be?"

After checking with the Test Administer, Detective Lee informed us, "The wait will be approximately an hour, give or take," and motioned with his hand indicating it wasn't an exact time.

There was a cafeteria in the building. My attorney asked me, "Would you like to go downstairs and have lunch? It's on me."

I responded with a polite, "No thank you." I was too nervous.

So, we sat on the hard wooden bench. On the other side of the wall were vending machines.

He said, "I am starving. I am going to see what I can get. Would you like for me to bring you something back?"

Again, I replied, "No, thank you, I just want to wait for the results."

He returned with two bags of peanuts and a soda. I witnessed the Test Administer leave his office with a manilla folder in his right hand as he briskly walked the corridor to locate Detective Lee. From a distance, I could see them conversing. Now I had to go to the bathroom. I was prancing back and forth on the bench, holding everything in. I couldn't wait any longer.

"I will be right back," I said, "I got to go to the lady's room."

When I returned, I saw the answer in the facial expression of my attorney. He gave me a thumbs up!

He said, "You passed with flying colors."

There was a big sigh of relief, silent prayer of, Thank You Jesus, tears of joy, and hugs with congratulatory expressions. My attorney offered to drop me off at home. I accepted with thanks. I was looking forward to getting home to see Ron. Our conversation included my appreciation for my attorneys' rendered service without charge.

He said to me, "Both myself and Detective Lee believed without a shadow of doubt, you did not meet the characteristics or profile of a criminal who would embezzle money." His final instructions were, "Wait for your employer to contact you. Then call me. Take care of yourself and your son."

It was about two weeks before my employer called me to let me know I was to appear before the U.S. Department of Labor, Commissioner's Review Office. My attorney met me that morning which seemed to be a shock to my employer (Mrs. Green).

The allegation of charges against me were that I had not adhered to the Bank's Policy and Procedures regarding an early day approved leave. She stated that this was a breach that had consequently caused a crime to occur, embezzlement of funds.

My attorney asked to review the Bank's Employee Handbook, which was made available by Mrs. Green, Bank President and C.E.O. No clause was found in the Employee Handbook with that language expressed by Mrs. Green.

Mrs. Green response was, 'The Bank's Underwriters are revising an upgraded version of the Employee Handbook that will include the correct verbiage on Policy and Procedures."

Without proper or compelling evidence supporting her claim, the Commissioner re-scheduled the next meeting in two weeks.

Because I had not been called back to work, I filed for unemployment benefits. Mrs. Green was fighting the request, she did not have grounds to fire me, so she was making my life as difficult as she could. What I didn't understand was, why?

# Chapter Twenty: Songs of Zion

*Walk with Me Lord*

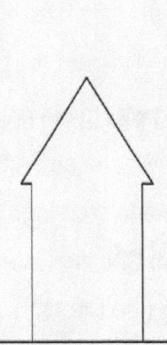

> *When someone lies on you, it feels like you have been condemned to a death sentence. When all the evidence seems to point in your direction, skeptics and non-believers turn from fellowship to foe, you search for just a ray of hope that someone will believe you. My heart was crushed and my soul sorrowful. Yet, the Lord was on my side. He did not allow the waters to overtake me, nor the fire to consume me, nor the arrows to come neigh me.*

The ride back home on the bus was more than I could take. The continued delays had drained my finances. I had started to get eviction notices. My credit card balances were behind. The only bills I paid were the utility payments. With winter on the horizon, that meant the holidays were approaching. Tears began to stream down my face. The lady sitting next to me noticed the pain I was in.

She said, "Oh, sweetheart, it can't be that bad. Things will work out."

Peering through my tears, I saw a kind face that matched her voice. Feeling overwhelmed and lifeless, I began to share with her my troubles. She patiently listened, as she reached in her purse and gave me a Kleenex tissue to dry my tears. She interrupted me just to let me know her stop was coming up shortly. I thanked her for listening and for the tissue. She placed her hand over mine and softly said, "My God will help you! I want you to call this number (local Catholic Diocese) and they will make an appointment to see you. I will pray for you and your son. May God's blessings rest upon you." She patted my hand and got off at the next stop.

Immediately, when I got home, I called the number and was given an appointment for the very next day at eleven thirty a.m. When I arrived at the Catholic Diocese, I was greeted by a friendly smile and greeting. She was the secretary who scheduled the appointment. She instructed me to, "Have a seat," she said pleasantly, "Mrs. Young (the Director) will meet with you shortly. Would you like a soda while you wait?"

"I politely said, "No." I was a little nervous. I never had this type of experience before. Asking for financial assistance was very difficult for me. I always believed that I could solve any situation that affected Ron and I. I didn't want anyone to have a negative opinion of me not being a good mother or provider. I strived diligently to be the best in whatever I was assigned too. This was a humbling experience. In the middle of my next thought, I heard my name called to join Mrs. Young. When I entered the room, Mrs. Young extended her hand, greeting me with, "I am so pleased to meet you." Then she asked, "How can we help you?"

I took a deep breath and decided to set my pride aside and let her know I was getting eviction notices and that my credit cards were gravely being diminished due to the lack of meeting the required minimum payment. As I described the events that brought me to this moment, tears began to swell up and drop from my eyes. Listening to my words left me feeling helpless. Although my situation was through no fault of my own, I felt sick in my body and ashamed of my financial position.

With compassionate eyes and kind words, Mrs. Young asked, "Do you have a copy of your apartment lease?"

I answered "No." But, I let her know that I could go home and get the lease.

"What is the phone number of your landlord?" She asked. After she spoke to the landlord, Mrs. Young pulled out a business check book from the top drawer of her desk. As she was writing, she said, "Take this check to your landlord. It is for the two months that you are in the rear and for next month. This should sustain you and your son until you are gainfully employed."

Tears were streaming down my face. I was in a state of awe!

She continued, "When your ship comes in, don't forget about us. Be at peace."

I thanked her repeatedly. As she walked me to the door, I hugged her and said, "I will remember the charity that was extended to me. I will bless back financially the love you gave to me as soon as I am able."

I received a phone call from my attorney. He said, "Marie, as you know, you have been cleared by the polygraph test taken at the police station." He continued, "You can return to your employment; however, I advise you to consider that option. The missing funds have not been recovered nor the person who took them have not been identified." He further stated with urgency, "Mrs. Green may still have harsh feelings towards you. It is possible she has tarnished your impeccable reputation among your co-workers.

Working in an atmosphere as such can cause unwarranted mistakes and irreparable mental damage to you. At this stage she cannot fire you without being susceptible to a lawsuit. Here are your options: you can return to work and receive your retroactive pay or resign and receive back unemployment benefits. The second option, unemployment, limits you from the time of application until the completion date of abirritation. Carefully consider my opinion. Keep in contact with me. Good luck to you and Ron in all your future endeavors."

I thanked my attorney for his investigative work as well as, helping me to prove my reputation innocence. I had so much to consider.

Surprisingly, the next day, Detective Lee called. After the salutations, Detective Lee asked if I would have lunch with him. I agreed! Friday of the same week that we had the conversation, I met with him for lunch. I was very curious why he wanted to meet with me. My nerves overwhelmed me at that moment. I only ordered a slice of strawberry pie and a cup of coffee.

While Detective Lee began to eat his cheeseburger and fries, he remarked, "You look great after the ordeal that you have been through. Have you decided if you are going to return to your employment?"

"No, I haven't decided yet. I spoke with my attorney, and he informed me of his recommendation. He said it would not be in my best interest to return to my employer. My dilemma with resigning would be my unemployment would cease. At the present time I have not secured other employment. I am concerned about the welfare of my son."

Detective Lee patiently waited for me to end my dialogue before he said, "We are continuing with our investigation and now have a strong suspect that has been identified in the case of the thirty-five hundred dollars embellished from the bank. We are aware that they are related to one of the bank's management personnel. We also know they have a drug problem. It is our belief they took the funds. Your early leave for that day gave them the opportunity to use you as an escape goat to cover up the crime. You were the perfect victim."

I was numb!

*Oh my God, my life was almost destroyed because of a lie!*

My heart was racing with fury! I wanted to do something bad to the suspected crook. I had suffered relentlessly as I tried to keep my sanity while pretending everything was okay. Tears were flowing.

Detective Lee further stated, "I agree with your attorney, it may be best that you do not return to your job. They may try to set you up, just to divert the ongoing investigation." He continued, "I have a friend who is head of Human Resources at one the larger department stores. I explained your situation to her, and she is willing to hire you on my recommendation. The salary is not what you were making, but it should sustain you until you find employment in your field."

I dried my tears and thanked him for his generosity, kindness, and the information regarding the on-going investigation. I acknowledged my interest in the department store position. This was the deciding factor I needed to submit my resignation to the bank. At that moment I felt as if a mountain had been removed from my shoulders. I could breathe! Prior to this moment, I was consumed with grief and hopefulness. Now, I felt my feet shift from sand to solid ground. I recalled the songs of Zion (*Walk with me Lord*) stir in my spirit.

When someone lies on you, it feels like you have been condemned to a death sentence. When all the evidence seems to point in your direction, skeptics and non-believers turn from fellowship to foe, you search for just a ray of hope that someone will believe you.

My heart was crushed and my soul sorrowful. Yet, the Lord was on my side. He did not allow the waters to overtake me, nor the fire to consume me, nor the arrows to come neigh me.

The Lord continued to daily extend His grace and mercy towards me. He heard my cry from the backside of the wilderness where there was darkness and delivered me from the jaws of the lion. I was wounded. Yet alive!

*Marie Jenkins', My Time*

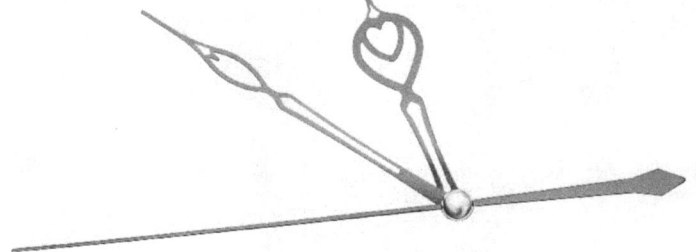

# Chapter Twenty-One: Unforsaken

Never Alone

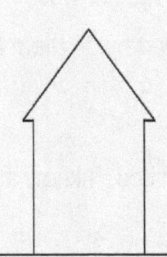

> *The weekend was painful without my son. The hours of the weekend were consumed with sleep. I needed a place to escape, where solitude and silence would embrace me. I yearned for covering that provided peace and protection. I had to reconnect with the one person who said, "I will never leave you nor forsake you." (Joshua 1:5 KJV)*

I was excited to get back home and share this information with Ron. Unknown to me, Ron had called my parents expressing his concern regarding my health. Before I could share the good news with him, he said, "Grandma wants you to call her as soon as you get in."

Heart racing and palms sweating, I called my mother. "Are you and Dad, ok?"

My mother responded, "We are fine. What about you?"

I asked her to clarify what she meant.

"Ron called overly excited, saying you were going to die. When I asked him why, he said, you were sad, crying all the time, not going to work, not eating, and losing weight." She asked again, "What is wrong?"

With tears in my eyes, chocking on every word, I began to tell her what had happened to me over the last several months. My mother was furious! She could not understand why I had not reached out to them for help.

"I did not want to burden you with my problems," I admitted. "I knew at some point I would recover. I had the Lord on my side."

We continued in conversation for about an hour.

Finally, my mother said, "Your father and I will come and get Ron until you get back on your feet. He can continue his schooling here with us."

At first, I rejected their proposal! Ron was mine. And I would continue to take care of him, just as I always had.

What convinced me was when my mother said, "This is only a temporary situation. He can call you and see you on the weekends. This will give you time to rebuild your life both physically and financially."

With the heaviness of heart, I agreed. When I shared the information with Ron, he was sad to leave me, yet excited to spend time in the country with his grandparents and uncle. When he left, I felt as if I could not make it; he was my primary reason for life.

I knew within myself, there was a little girl yearning to be released. She had found solace in the comfort of yesterday's innocence. Afraid of the unknown, I joined her. Warmth, acceptance, and candor where her covering. I could hear laughter with the breeze of a warm summer day. I could dream of a future uncluttered, unscared by evil. There, I could live in purpose without reservations, heartaches, disappointments, or grief.

I felt so alone! I had become isolated as if I was abandoned on an island which was a combination of my life's experiences. I felt alone for most of my life. With the walls I had built, they not only kept out uncomfortable situations, but they also isolated me from personal growth. Often, I felt as if my life experiences positioned me on an island, abandoned and fearful. I realized I had to "do or die." Options were limited. I had to change my thought process. I had to believe in me. I remapped the directions regarding my current position and posture. I encouraged myself to energize strategize, mobilize and P.U.S.H. (pray until something happens). My tenacity to "be better" drove my faith to another level. This time I had to step beyond. But each direction of the winds dismantled my coverings except for my faith, which was restored by God.

The weekend was painful without my son. The hours of the weekend were consumed with sleep. I needed a place to escape, where solitude and silence would embrace me. I yearned for covering that provided peace and protection. I had to reconnect with the one person who said, "I will never leave you nor forsake you." (Joshua 1:5 KJV)

Comforted by my thoughts of the Lord, sleep would finally come.

Monday morning greeted me with the sound of bells. The alarm clock indicted six o'clock a.m. This was the first day of orientation with the department store. I was hired over the phone thanks to the recommendation of Detective Lee.

Before I entered the building, I mailed my resignation letter to my previous employer. It felt so good!

My appointment today was with Ms. Blake. She was the Human Resources. Director. Meeting her was delightful. She was stately and impressive. She was poised and gracious as she extended her right hand to me, "Good morning, Marie, I have heard wonderful things concerning you. It is my pleasure to welcome you to our organization." She went on to say, "Fill out the paperwork then return it to me. After company policies have been addressed, you will get your assignment."

I started that day in sales. Which I hated! It only took a few weeks before I was promoted to an Administrative Management position. At that time, I had an Associate Degree in Business. After about six months on the job, Ms. Blake called me to her office. I was a little nervous.

She greeted me with a smile and said, "I want to commend you on your work performance. I have a friend who is recruiting qualified persons to fill Teller positions. I know your background is in banking. Although I would hate to lose you, I thought about you and expressed to him that I would share the information with you."

My heart was beating so fast. I was excited. I responded with a joyous, "Yes."

I expressed to Ms. Blake how grateful I was to be considered. The interview would be in two days. That evening Detective Lee called. He asked me how things were going. I felt confident enough to share with him the events that had taken place within the last six months and the excitement of the interview with the bank.

He said, "I have faith in you that you will get the position."

I thanked him for his support. We talked for about an hour. Before we hung up, he said, "I would like to take you to dinner." There was a period of silence between us. "Did I hear a yes?" He asked. I was so overwhelmed by his proposal.

I answered, "Yes."

The date was set. I was nervous; it was several hours before I fell asleep. I kept thinking and thanking God for the turning of good things coming into my life.

Thursday morning, I was awake before the alarm clock went off. I said my prayers while I was in the shower. Today, I would interview with Mr. Horowitz for a Teller position with the bank (Rivers Flow).

When I arrived at the corporate office, I was immediately received by Mr. Horowitz the Human Resources Director. The interview was in-depth. After about thirty minutes, Mr. Horowitz shook my hand, escorted me to the door and stated in a monotone voice, "Someone will be in touch with you, soon."

When I left the office, I was not sure if I had the position. I was looking for a positive verbal or non-verbal sign. There was none to be heard or seen! I returned to the department store, sadden. When I took my lunch break, I informed Ms. Blake about the outcome of the interview.

She encouraged me, "I am positive that things will work out on your behalf."

With that, I grabbed a tuna sandwich and soda and finished my lunch.

When I returned home, I was sitting on needles and pins knowing that an answer would not come before tomorrow. The bank was closed. I picked up the phone and called my mother. I updated her on all the current events that were happening in my life. After I was finished, I asked to speak with Ron. (Knowing my mother, she would have talked until the wee hours of the morning.) I was overjoyed to catch up with Ron's schooling and sports. He had made both the basketball and football teams. I was a proud mama! He didn't seem like he missed me as much as I missed him. He was happy.

Ron had adjusted not only to country living; he was surrounded by cousins. There was no threat of bullying, as opposed to defending himself against others in the city. Again, I was sad. He finished the conversation and handed the phone back to my mother. For the next hour or two, I was informed about all the neighborhood gossip, and why she was still mad at my father for catering to the church parishioner, which had exhausted her last nerve. This was a never-ending story! Hearing her woes made me temporarily forget about my troubles. After an exhausting conversation, I was ready for bed and couldn't get there fast enough. I had no trouble falling asleep.

Monday morning, I went to work as scheduled. My body was there fulfilling duty, but my thoughts were inundated with the need to know if I was the chosen candidate for the bank position. And if I was, when would they inform me. My shift was over, and I was on my way back home. I was feeling sad. It was after four o'clock p.m., the bank was closed.

*Perhaps tomorrow I will hear something.* I thought.

Well, Tuesday came and went and still no word. I was beginning to lose hope. I was sure the interview went well. In my mind, I revisited the interview process with Mr. Horowitz. The pictorial of that day was vivid. My posture was straight, I maintained good eye contact, wore a dark two-piece suit, only answered questions when asked, and left my professional Business Resume. Now, I was overly concerned regarding my possibilities. The weight of being on the fence, caused me not to be very talkative. This evening, Saturday, Detective Lee was taking me to dinner. I hoped my company would not reflect sadness.

Detective Lee took me to a beautiful restaurant with a scenic view overlooking Pittsburgh. It was breathtaking. The sun had just set and the sky cascaded with various forms shaped by clouds. The panoramic picturesque range was vivid. I could see mountain tops, clusters of homes reflecting the look of doll houses. From my position, I could also see roads and highways running until they connected with the sky. Trains and trucks, with the power of vision, resembled the same ones placed under the Christmas tree for every little boy.

Detective Lee was a gentleman. He opened doors, pulled out the chair, walked on the outside of the sidewalk and assisted me with ordering dinner. I felt like I was on a merry-go-round; experiencing sights of great images; feeing the mood of a romantic ambience; smelling exotic aromas coming from the kitchen. Yet, I was extremely sorrowful. I pondered over the reality that this night will end!

The secure financial future for Ron and I have not even begun. I had so many regrets. If only I could go back and change the direction of time. I did share with Detective Lee, the events of the bank interview as well as the daily occurrences of my job with the department store.

He encouraged me to have faith in the process. Whatever that meant! I smiled, graciously.

After dinner, he drove me home.

"You were a lovely dinner date. I had a great time. Again, keep your head up!"

I thanked him for a wonderful time. I also conveyed my appreciation for the help and assistance he provided me. As I was getting out of the car, he said, "My first name is Robert. You may call me Bob, with no Mr. or Detective attached."

I smiled and said thank you. I will. Good night, Bob.

His final words, "I will call you tomorrow, good night, Marie."

Once I got into my flannel pj's, I called my mother.

I gave her a blow-by-blow description of my evening. She detected the lack of luster in my voice and asked me, "Did you not enjoy your date with the detective?"

"Yes," I said, and I began to correct her. "His first name is Robert. But he said I can call him Bob."

We both laughed as I continued to share. I asked my mom to give me a full report on Ron. How were his grades? Was he doing his share of chores? Patiently, she responded.

"Ron is keeping up his grade average to stay on the Basketball and Football teams. He takes out the trash. He helps me with the dishes after dinner. When Granddad cuts the grass or does odds and ends at the church, Ron sticks with him. He's no trouble. We know he misses and worries about you."

It was a good report. I was comforted to know he was doing ok. It was painful not being able to share with him the moments my parents were experiencing.

We both said our good nights.

I set the alarm clock for seven thirty a.m. My ride for Sunday School and morning service would arrive at nine o'clock a.m.

# Chapter Twenty-Two: The Breath of God

Boundless Love

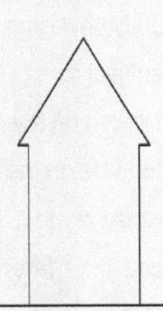

*I discovered love has no boundaries. It swells, grows, increases, cultivates, nourishes, incubates and aids development of one's self. With God's wisdom, my mom and their dad encouraged me as I instilled these origins with the precious vessels entrusted to me, my children. Motherhood empowered me to be better. It matured my thinking, actions, and decisions. It expanded thoughts of future mobility.*

Once back home from church, Ms. Anne called. "Come on over and have dinner with us. I have new movies to watch and afterwards you can tell me about your date." She said laughing.

"Ok," I agreed. "I will see you soon!"

I found a long old sleeve shirt to cover my arms. The eczema was continually and progressively getting worse. It didn't seem like the cortisone cream was helping. Dr. Farney continued to prescribe .25 mg cortisone pills for the treatment of allergic reactions, skin conditions, and the immune system. Often, I would not take them. I would skip the daily doses which could last up to a week at a time. I had read the information regarding debilitating side effects that could protentional result in sterilization and damage to the nervous system. I was advised by my physician not to abruptly stop taking the prescription on my own. But, to confer with her on a step-down treatment that would end the use of the medication.

The skin on my body was hurting from scratching. My body's reaction to age maturity worsens with dark scaring and thickening. My physician not only prescribed a lightening cream, but I was also subject to injections to thin the thicken areas. These areas were located on my arms and the creases of my legs. The area most affected was on the back of my neck. It was elevated. There were nights I would cry to relieve the pain in my heart. My self-esteem had dwindled like a fallen leaf; lifeless, brittle and dried up.

After I applied another application of the cortisone cream, I put on the shirt and went to Ms. Annie's house for dinner.

Once I began to eat and socialize with Ms. Annie, her guests and her kids, I felt so much better. After we watched a couple of action-packed rental movies, Ms. Annie and I were the last ones standing. I began to share with her the highlights of my date with Detective Lee (Bob).

She was elated and asked, "When is he going to take you out again?"

I laughed, and answered, "I don't know. Soon, I hope!"

Tired and sleepy, I gave Ms. Annie a kiss on her cheek, thanked her for dinner and the plate she made me to take home. Soon after I got into my flannel pj's the telephone rang.

Yes, it was Bob. The conversation was brief, but not without a consensual calendar date for our next outing.

I arrived at work Monday morning feeling a little sad. I had not heard anything from the bank. Around two thirty that afternoon, Ms. Blake called for me. She wanted to see me in her office before my shift was over. When I arrived at her office, she had a pleasant smile on her face. As if she had won an all-expense Las Vegas trip. She said, "I have good news for you, Mr. Horowitz would like for you to call him before you leave today."

"Ok," I responded.

Ms. Blake further stated, "You can use my phone. His phone number is written on the scratch pad. I will step out to give you privacy."

I thanked her for the generosity. I could feel the butterflies in my stomach. My hand was shaking as I dialed the phone number. A women's voice identified the organization in which I connected with. She continued, "How may I help you or direct you?"

I asked to speak with Mr. Horowitz.

She responded, "Hold on, I will connect you."

Finally, I heard his voice, "Hi Marie, I was expecting your call. How are you today?" There was a friendly overture in his voice.

*Could this mean?*

I responded to Mr. Horowitz as friendly as he did and professionally as I could, "I am doing very well. I hope your day has been a good one."

There was a chuckle and response, "I am having a fantastic day! I have filled the Teller position offered by the bank if you agree to accept."

I know there was a ten second delay from me before I answered. When I did speak, I kept saying, "Yes," over and over until Mr. Horowitz said, "Thank you Marie. Welcome aboard! We are delighted to have you on our Team." Then he asked, "When can you start? I have already spoken with Ms. Blake. She needs you until the end of the week. So, if you can start on Monday, we are in agreement."

I was swimming in scattered emotions as I said, "Yes."

I asked Mr. Horowitz, what was the starting time.

He responded, "Meet me in my office at eight o'clock a.m. There will be forms you will need to fill out. Then I will go over the Employee Handbook with you and escort you to your station."

When I hung up, I was thanking God for His favor towards me. I would be able to financially take care of us. Ron can come home. I thanked Mr. Horowitz for his vote of confidence. I couldn't wait until I got home.

First, I called my mother to share with her the good news. She was delighted! She said, "Prayer works." I asked to speak to Ron.

Mom said, "He is still at football and basketball practice."

"Tell him to call me as soon as he gets in," I said excitedly, "and tell dad the good news too."

My mother and I didn't talk long, I told her I had a few more people to share the good news with. Without hesitation, I headed over to Annie's apartment. When she saw my smile wider than an eighty-eight Steinway piano, she knew I had got the job!

"Oh, happy day!" Annie said. "I just brewed a fresh pot of coffee. Would you like a cup?"

I nodded, yes.

I began to tell her the good news. Our coffee had become cold. As Annie refilled our cups, I noticed we had been talking for quite some time. I let Annie know that I had to leave. There was one more phone call I was waiting on. We hugged as I said good night.

When I got back to my apartment, I slipped into my pj's.

The telephone woke me up. It was Bob. I was groggy when I told him about the good news. I would be a full-time employee with benefits. He congratulated me saying, "I knew you would ace it."

I wanted to continue in the celebratory conversation, but I was falling asleep.

Bob said, "I will call you tomorrow, good-night."

The remaining days of the week seemed to go bye so quickly.

Saturday morning arrived with a flurry of activity. It was cleaning day, grocery shopping day, and mother-daughter catch-up talk time. And I had to be ready at six o'clock for dinner. Bob was taking me to dinner. The engagement served a dual purpose. It was our second date along with the celebration of a new job.

When he picked me up, Bob presented me with a dozen red roses. I could hardly contain myself. We went to a newly opened restaurant in downtown Pittsburgh. It had once been a movie theater. The conversion was remarkable. The first floor was a completely lighted dance floor. The colors would change according to the beat of the music. On the left side of the dance floor was a bar and on the right side were large, cushioned lounge chairs. Between the chairs, some grouped in two's, threes and four's, stood decorative flickering candles, setting a passionate scene. We were escorted to the second floor. The host escorted us to our table. He pulled out the chair for me, placed a white linen napkin on my lap, and presented me with the house menu. Bob adjusted himself accordingly and was given a menu, as well. I feasted on baked fish, with a lemon sauce, baked potato, and steamed carrots. Bob ordered surf and turf. It came with a baked potato and asparagus.

After dinner and conversation, we went downstairs and danced. I had a wonderful evening. Before I got out the car that night, he said, "I will call you tomorrow. I enjoyed your company. You are a dynamic dancer. Good night."

I thanked him for the evening and said good night.

Monday morning, I woke up before the alarm went off. It was a day that came with new beginnings. I could begin to exhale to a future certain of promise and fulfilled purpose. I could continue to build on a foundation that promised financial stability. I could independently undergird dreams, aspirations and endeavors for Ron and myself.

I know the Lord heard my prayers. I felt the breath of God moving across my being moving me much like the waves move across the ocean cresting in harmony with shore, resending for a new refreshing.

After orientation, I met with the District Manager (Mr. Rucker) and the other employees whom I would be working with. My exceptional work ethics on behalf of customer relations and team cooperation, increased my end of year raises. My overall performance encouraged Mr. Rucker to promote me to a Financial Administrator. The position expanded my growth in financial decisions. I attended the American Institute of Banking, Pittsburgh, Pennsylvania, with completion and Certification.

During this process Bob and I were engaged to be married. I was happy! Ron liked Bob as well as my mother and father. We were married in November days before Thanksgiving at my father's church,

Burgettstown, Pennsylvania. We were joined in holy matrimony by my father, Reverend Samuel Williams, Pastor. Ron gave me away. The ceremony was small and intimate attended by family, church members, and friends.

I didn't think I could have any more children. The steroids I was prescribed to take ever since I was a young teenager, were known to cause sterilization as a possible side effect. I had great aspirations looking forward to Ron's graduation and college entry. (He had numerous athletic scholarships offered from universities across the country.) However, an alternate course had already developed; I was pregnant. This time, it would be a little girl! I was excited and frightful. These emotions were mutually intertwined. When I informed my employer, they gave me a baby shower that looked like a baby department store. The only thing missing was the golden spoon, which her God mother purchased.

I had already given my baby girl a name before she was born, while she was in my womb, Michele. She would also be called Mikki. This would be her nick name. When she got older, her friends also called her, Shell, Gucci and Sha. I always thought having a nick name was so cool. I didn't have one growing up. All my friends had nick names. Some of them had two. I am convinced, not being given a nickname made me feel excluded.

The first time I held Michele in my arms was the most delightful experiences I had encountered. I was overwhelmed with emotions that caused tears of joy and gratefulness to occur. That maternal instinct of love was present. The amazing fact was I could love this little one the same as I did for my first born. Michele only weighed five pounds, four ounces. She was so tiny and adorable. Her cries sounded like whimpers. They were so cute. I had two children I adored. Then after twenty months, Michael was born.

I discovered love has no boundaries. It swells, grows, increases, cultivates, nourishes, incubates and aids development of one's self. With God's wisdom, my mom and their dad encouraged me as I instilled these origins with the precious vessels entrusted to me, my children. Motherhood empowered me to be better. It matured my thinking, actions, and decisions. It expanded thoughts of future mobility.

After the birth of Michael, my husband and I decided that I would come home full time. When I turned in my resignation, again my co-workers planned a baby shower designed for a little prince. Knowing that resigning would be the last time I would be connected to co-workers I had built personal relationships with, hit me hard. My last day was bitter-sweet. hugs, kisses, and tears where the climate of the office.

Two days later I went into labor. Michael was a pretty boy baby. He had locks of curly black hair. My heart made room for the little guy.

It was a challenge, one toddler being potty trained, an infant and a teenager graduating from high school into the society of young manhood. There was never a dull moment in my life. Even though it was rigorous and stressful at times, it was completely fulfilling and rewarding. The trajectory of my life took a turn from previous plans.

I had several endeavors after Ron went to college to continue a career in business finance. My desire was reconfirmed to be a full-time mother to Michele and Michael. At no time did I regret my decision. I was able to relive youth as I did with Ron. Of course, there were cultural changes. Technology evolved into Pac Man and Mario maze chase video games that could be operated by four-year-old little boys and girls. Roller blades was all the crave, replacing inline skates. Roller blade wheels were positioned as a single frame in the middle of the skate. Whereas, line skate wheels had two horizontal frames.

Parents were challenged regarding safety. Of course, we gave into the pressure. We padded elbows, knees and hands, applied a helmet and let nature take her course. I have had more than my share of big wheels, Flintstone mobile, and finally, a motor operated Jeep and Barbie car.

Most holiday celebrations were held at our house. We had a play gym and plenty of room for sidewalk games. My parents visited often. My skin was clearing up and I was happy even though I went from a size ten to a full body size woman's twelve. I re-dedicated my life to the Lord and my husband became an Elder in the church. I was a hands-on mom with the kids as their interest expanded in various areas: softball, music, dance, girl scouts, church youth related activities, parties, field trips, yearly Debutante Balls, summer programs, traveling choirs, just to name a few. Even as the kids matriculated through the educational system, I was a supporter.

Some of my fondest memories were through interaction and participation with the children. As they got older and my husband retired from the Police Department, we were able to devote more time to my parents and the activities of the church; both thirty miles away. While the kids were still in school, Saturdays were spent in the country, Burgettstown, PA., with the family.

We would pack lunches, take toys, while tools bundled and arranged were placed in the back of the van.

*Photo 4 Michael & Michele - first day of school*

*Marie Jenkins', My Time*

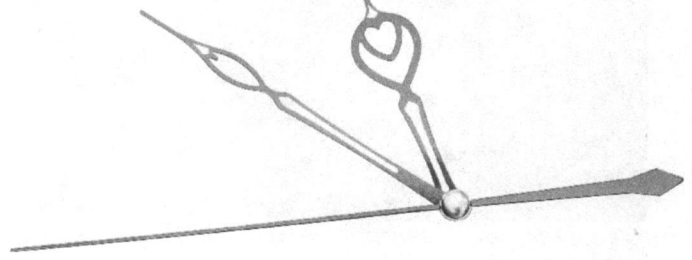

# Chapter Twenty-Three: Miracle

*God's Word*

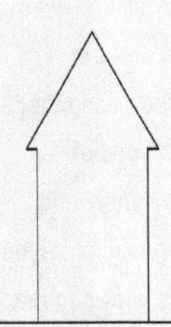

*As I left the hospital, I felt like I was sinking on a ship without sails. I couldn't see stars because darkness covered the skies. The moon hid in the blackness, while the compass dial moved uncontrollably seeking its position. My skin responded to the stress and anxiety I was experiencing. I was having trouble sleeping at night. My eyes twitched uncontrollably. My appetite was limited to my desire for food. I was losing weight and didn't feel very well. I stayed tired and sleepy.*

The church and my parents' home were in a small town, Francis Mine. Both church and their home were across the road from each other. The community was small, bi-racial, and friendly. Everyone knew the families of others. The children had space to ride bikes, play double Dutch jump robe, baseball, relay races, and fly kites. They made friends with many of the children. There was also an abundance of cousins available for play and interaction. The older boys would often start a game of basketball.

My mother and I would sit on the porch and watch. My father and husband would be engaged working on completing projects and beautifying the church. My brothers, Ron and the men in the neighborhood would carry their tools to the sound where hammering and sawing was heard. The evening hours uncovered hungry souls both young and old. Our family members (except the kids who were pizza lovers), were avid Kentucky fried Chicken lovers. The Colonel was the Saturday and Sunday after church, go too.

The fellowship with all who were present, including the children, was amazing. Color barriers did not present any disruptions. We ate together, worshipped together, worked together, and had each other's well-being at heart. The tranquility among us became a bond of connectivity. My parents were respected within the community and beyond. Sunday worship morning service drew congregants far beyond the borders of Francis Mine. My father (the Pastor) was known to many as a Christian gentleman.

When Michael started school (Kindergarten) I volunteered every day at the school to be near him and Michele (second grader). I held the secretarial position with the Parent Teacher Association (PTA). Halfway through the school year, I was offered a part time secretarial position with the school district. I accepted.

*I might as well get paid for my volunteerism.*

I would drop the kids off to their class, park, and begin my day in the same building. The part-time position became full time shifting the work site to the District Administration Building. The morning routine remained the same. Dad would pick the kids up after school. The new position was rewarding and challenging with movement. Opportunity allowed me to operate in multiple departments within the School District: Tax Office, Data Input, Office of K-12th Registration, Administrative Secretary for School District Therapist, District Vocational Secretary, High School Curriculum Coordinator and Secretary to the High School Principal. There were days I thought I could effectively run the school district.

These were just passing thoughts.

Each day when I would get home, I noticed my husband was moping around the house. To my eye, he was losing weight, while getting darker. I questioned him to a fault, which sometimes led to heated arguments.

"I am fine!" He continued to say. "If there was something wrong, I would tell you."

My eyes told my heart that was not the case. But I left it alone. Until the next time. I did not think my assessments were unfounded. One morning when I dropped the kids off to school, I continued to the grocery store to pick up a few groceries. When I returned home, Bob was sitting at the kitchen table sweating profusely. He had his head in his hand, groaning with slurred speech. I was so frightened. I couldn't make any sense of what he was trying to tell me. I ask him if he wanted me to take him to the hospital. He shook his head, yes. I noticed he could not get up on his own from his seated position. I offered assistance by under griding his left arm, instructing him to push from the table, as I tried to pull him up. We attempted this technique several times until I knew it was hopeless. When I looked closely at the right side of his head, there was a big gash. (Later, I was told he had fallen in the bathroom, hitting his head on the side of the toilet.) Immediately, I called 911, requesting for an ambulance. While waiting, I put up the groceries that needed to be refrigerated or frozen. From outside I could hear the ambulance backing into the driveway.

Two Paramedics placed a neck brace on him, then placed him on the gurney. I followed the ambulance to the hospital.

At the Emergency desk, I was asked questions regarding Bob's injuries. I wasn't very helpful disclosing what had occurred. Therefore, it seemed liked hours before I was able to see him or talk with the doctor. They ran all kind of test to make sure there were not any internal injuries.

His report was not good.

Bob had suffered a severe head concussion, as well as a stroke. They kept him for further testing. The doctor asked me a series of questions regarding his health, his daily movements and diet. I answered to the best of my ability.

The doctor said, "It will be a few hours before he would be taken to his room. If you have errands to attend to, now will be a good time to do them."

*Marie Jenkins', My Time*

I was overwhelmed with anxiety! When I looked at the time, I panicked. The kids would be getting out of school in twenty minutes. Driving beyond the legal speed limit and prayed that every time I accelerated the gas pedal, I would not be stopped by a Police officer or get behind a school bus. The Lord heard my prayer! I also asked Him for forgiveness for not obeying speed limits. Once the kids were with me, I told them about their father. After dinner, I dropped the kids off at Anne's house.

When I reached my husband's room, he did not look good. His mouth was twisted. His speech was slurred, and he was grumpy. I tried hard not to show my emotions. I wanted to cry! I didn't really know what to say. I kept starring at him. My brain was on overload. My thoughts were all over the place.

I kept thinking; *our lives are going to change. Bob will never be the same again.* I asked myself more questions: *Will I be a good, efficient caretaker? Will Bob be able to walk without assistance?*

I felt selfish. After all Bob was the one suffering. Yet, I was drowning in my woes. Conversation between us was limited. I watched television with him for a while before I knew it was time for me to leave. His demeaner indicated he was not comfortable with me there. I would not be able to speak with the doctor until morning. I put away the clothing and toiletries I had brought. I asked him if there was anything else needed? He shook his head, no. I kissed him on the forehead and whispered, "I love you."

Looking into his eyes revealed profound sadness.

As I left the hospital, I felt like I was sinking on a ship without sails. I couldn't see stars because darkness covered the skies. The moon hid in the blackness, while the compass dial moved uncontrollably seeking its position. My skin responded to the stress and anxiety I was experiencing. I was having trouble sleeping at night. My eyes twitched uncontrollably. My appetite was limited to my desire for food. I was losing weight and didn't feel very well. I stayed tired and sleepy.

The next day, I thought I would be able to speak with the doctor. He had just left making his morning rounds. He did leave instructions on how my husband was to be cared for once he left the hospital. His stay would be extended with therapy. When I walked into the hospital room, I was not greeted with warmth. Bob's head was hung down not willing to have interactions with me. So, I read to him the instruction the doctor ordered on his behalf. He did not show any emotions one way or the other. After the nurse administered his meds and housekeeping changed his bed, I told him I would be back that evening.

With a faint whimper, he said, "I will call you when it is time for my departure."

I couldn't believe what I heard. If it wasn't such a struggle for him to speak, I would have asked him to repeat what was previously said. I didn't know if I was angry or insulted. Probably both! I complied with his instructions. I waited on his phone call asking me to come and get him.

The children were overjoyed to see their father. Not so much with me. Our greetings to each other were casual. Each day carried numerous challenges.

Through prayer, God's Word, gospel music along with the prayers of the Saints, I was able to accomplish one day at a time. Bob pushed his body to exhaustion to be able to walk on his own without the assistance of the cane. He was determined to walk with the full potential of erected posture.

Within the span of a year, Bob had accomplished his goal, his prayers were not only heard but answered. He no longer needed the assistance of his cane. He walked up-right with only a slight limp. His speech was clear and concise. He was a miracle!

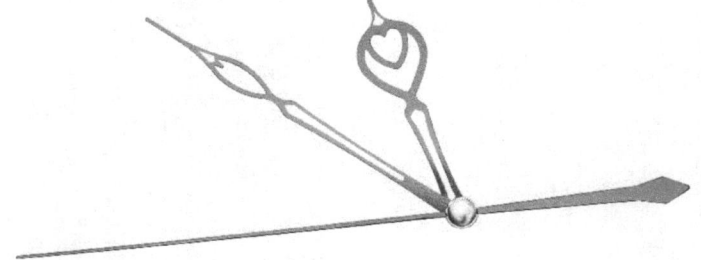

*Marie Jenkins', My Time*

# Chapter Twenty-Four: Shut Down

*Not Normal*

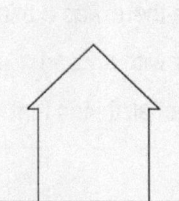

*I was being smothered by my thoughts, as well as conversations circulating around the table. I was aware but distant. It's as if I had been placed in a glass cylinder, I could hear, see, and feel; yet my ability to reason had shut down.*

Little by little I noticed a change in Bob's personality and my response to the change.

He was short tempered, combative at times, and wanted to be left to his own company. I excused much of the behavior to his illness. Healthy communications within our family members were eroding. He gave short uncompassionate responses. I was changing! My temper was short, I couldn't embrace pressures from a normal day's activities like previously. I was off balance, not knowing how to regain the center, or the bounce. Bob's spirit were deteriorating, and neither one of us maintained a high priority of eating.

Church fellowship, visitation with my parents, and Bob's assisting my dad with church renovations dwindled from numerous visits per week down to once a week, on Sundays. Daily schedules changed.

The transformation of Bob's responsibilities shifted, aligning me with headship. The position was not hard, just, challenging. Prior to his illness, Bob addressed the financial responsibilities of our family. I recalculated my daily schedule to include grocery shopping, picking up the kids from school, and caretaker, while working full time. There were days when I felt so alone. I wouldn't complain. Often, when I spoke to my mother, she would ask me how things were. Since there was a thirty miles distance between us, I didn't want to burden her with my sad stories. I kept the faith, believing the Lord would correct all things that were disjointed.

Throughout the five years of my husband's illness, I noticed his impending demise. It was settling yet noticeable. He was losing quite a bit of body weight, along with darkening of his skin color. I was not invited to his visits to the doctor. This made me very suspicious.

The last family Thanksgiving dinner hosted at our home would be the last time our family would gather for a holiday celebration. Bob struggled to prepare the dinner with all the traditional fixings.

As always, I oversaw the Sweet Potato pies. I had learned to master the recipe. Individual eyes would constantly shift to the buffet for reassurance of their presence. Bob cooked macaroni and cheese casserole, collard greens, honey ham, black eye peas, homemade rolls, beef roast, homemade mashed potatoes/ brown gravy, and lemonade.

The family dinned sufficiently with plates to take home. Even at dinner I noticed Bob did not eat much. Later he revealed to me that his elbow and lower arm was in excruciating pain. I found out he suffered with

Rheumatoid arthritis which affected body joints. At that moment, if someone would have asked me how I felt, I would have busted into uncontrollable tears.

He was physically suffering; the kids and I were emotionally suffering.

After the Thanksgiving gathering, Bob began to decrease in his health. When the kids and I would get home, he would be sitting in the wing back chair in the living room in pain and silence. Each day I experienced a profound anxious alarm of apprehensive fear. These feelings pressed me to have a conversation with my mother.

Low and behold, when I began to share with her my situation, she said, "Last week I called to tell son-in-law how much we enjoyed spending Thanksgiving with the family and how much I ate. I told him the food was delicious, and Dad and I are still feasting on the ham sent home with us." She further stated, "He chuckled and said how much he enjoyed not only the company but preparing the food for the family."

It was what she divulged next that caused me to re-adjust my sitting position.

"I asked him how he was feeling and was he still taking his medicine and he told me that he had stopped taking the medicine and was waiting on the Lord to heal him. He said he was concerned about you and the kids. He said you look so tired and sad. And I told him, she is very worried about your weight loss. She can't understand why you don't have an appetite, and why she can't go with you to your doctor appointments." My mother said Bob didn't respond so she moved on to another subject.

Our conversation didn't make me feel any better. Nor did it answer questions. My mother did tell me, "If Bob can't get up out of the bed, and he has an accident while you are at work, criminal neglect charges can be filed against you."

"What?" I asked in shock. I tried several times to convince him to let me take him to the hospital. Each time he refused. I have even called for an ambulance. The dispatcher told me, "If your husband is coherent and refuses our services, we cannot take him against his will."

"So, what am I supposed to do," I asked my mother. "I must work!"

I was so up-set! I couldn't even think rational. That night before bed I tried to engage Bob in conversations regarding his health, doctor appointments and the effect his behavior was having on me. I showed him where my skin was breaking out. At that moment I felt like everything was closing in on me. My thoughts were racing in various directions. Nothing had a rhyme or reason. Our lives were disjointed and fragmented.

The fact that he would not communicate with me, made the situation even more stressful.

After a while I accepted the non-interactions.

As I reflect on the week before his death, his behavior had become erratic.

One evening when I was changing bed linen, I found three of his back teeth hidden on the nightstand that had come out. When I approached him regarding this, he just shrugged his shoulders without comment. This was another faze he was trying to conceal in order to hide his true condition.

Saturday afternoon in his weakened condition, he came down the steps in a seated position, sliding one step at time until he reached the living room. That evening after dinner the kids helped him back upstairs. Later, I helped him get in bed and I continued my routine, getting the kids and I clothes ready for church in the morning.

My sleep that night was restless.

I got up the next morning (Sunday), with the sound of the alarm. Before going into the bathroom, I woke up the kids. When I returned to get dressed, the kids were downstairs watching cartoons. I called for them to take their showers and then get breakfast. In the meanwhile, I began to get dressed. As I was putting on my blouse, I began to speak with Bob.

I told him that the kids and I would be home after the benediction was said. There was no verbal response from him. I thought he was awake, resting with his hands behind his head, eyes closed. I left the bedroom to fuss at the kids to get dressed and get a bowl of cereal before it was time to leave.

When I returned to the bedroom, I sat on the bed to put my shoes on. I was rambling on about the kids making us late for Sunday school. I turned to him and asked him if he wanted breakfast before we left. I let him know we would not get out of service before one o'clock.

It was not eight thirty in the morning. Bob was still in the same posture as previous. I became furious with his non-response. So, I stood up, placed both hands on my hips and asked, "Did you hear me?"

Again, there was no response. So, I walked around to his side of the bed, touched him to shake him, no response. I was so agitated, I touched him again, this time on his arm. He was cold as ice!

By this time, I was screaming at him, shaking him, asking, "What is wrong?"

The Lord let me know, he had departed from life. I kept starring at him. He looked so peaceful! I put both hands to my mouth and let out a terrorizing scream. I backed out of the bedroom, tears flowing from my eyes. I must have taken two steps at a time to reach the first floor of the house. I hurried to the telephone and dialed 911. The operator answered the phone and asked, "911, what is your emergency?"

I tried to answer in a calm voice because the kids where in the next room. I said, "Please send an ambulance. My husband's body is ice cold, and he is not responding to my touch or verbal commands."

The operator asked, "When did you first notice his condition?"

I told her, "Just a few minutes ago"

"Did you try to administer mouth to mouth resuscitation?"

At that point, I lost my calm composure! I became erratic and yelled at the top of my voice, "He is dead! Please send someone, please.!"

Before I could complete the call with the 911 operator, I heard the kids going up stairs, calling, "Daddy," over and over.

The operator requested our home address, while dispatching paramedics. I dropped the phone and ran upstairs after the kids. Michele and Michael were shaking him, tears were flowing from both their eyes, as they franticly called for his response. I felt I was living in a suspense movie. I ran to the other side of the bed frantically encouraging them to stop and return downstairs.

They asked, "What's wrong with Dad?"

I answered, "He's gone."

They continued questioning me, "Where is he? Gone where?"

I said, "He is dead!"

My heart was beating rapidly. When I looked in their faces, it was as if the earth stood still, and time had frozen.

He is now with the Lord. I never imagined I would be delivering such a message. As we left the room, we all were crying, asking God, "Why?"

Three of us sat huddled together in the family room, comforting each other. I was so overwhelmed. I didn't know who to call. My parents were thirty miles away from us. Ron was now married with children. I called Ron. This was the week he had Army drills and was out of town. My thoughts were searching for a name that I could get in touch with. The first person to reach the house was my daughter-n-law. She sat with the kids and consoled them. I called the church we fellowshipped with and asked to speak with Mother Shields. When I heard her voice, I immediately said, "I need you, please come, he's gone!"

She said, "I am on my way."

Just as I hung up the phone, there was heavy knocking at the back door. It was the Police. There were two officers dispatched. Because Bob's death occurred in the house, the police officers asked me a multitude of questions. They requested several of his personal items including his medicine and driver's license.

Ron had made it to the house by then. He sat with me as I was being questioned by the Police. Somewhere in the conversation, the coroner truck arrived. After they removed Bob's body, Ron went up to the bedroom and cleaned up. I am blessed to be able to remember and chart the events of that dreadful day.

One by one, my Pastor came, my parents came, several church members and those who had heard of Bob's death came, also. So many were kind, concerned, and consoling. I don't really remember much of the conversations. My thoughts were fixed on my husband's body lying in the mortuary, refrigerated. These thoughts were playing over and over in my head.

The coroner determined that Bob died from Congestive Heart Failure.

I was being smothered by my thoughts, as well as conversations circulating around the table. I was aware but distant. It's as if I had been placed in a glass cylinder, I could hear, see, and feel; yet my ability to reason had shut down.

Little did I know, I was in shock!

Because of the state of being I existed in, years later I discovered my female reproductive system ceased to be. I didn't go through Menopause. Some say, "this was a blessing."

I knew it was not normal.

*Marie Jenkins', My Time*

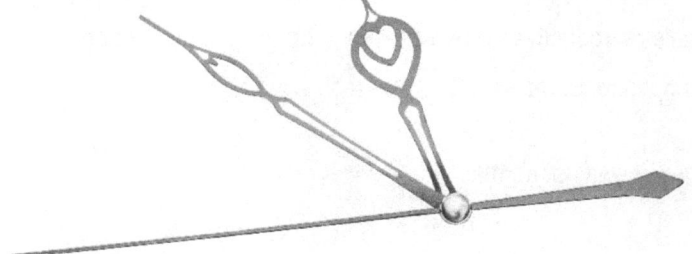

# Chapter Twenty-Five: Another Ending

*Until Resurrection Day*

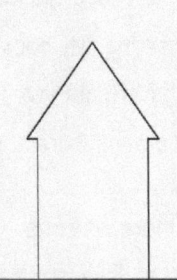

*Saturday came like any other day of the week. I woke up drained. After the kids and I got dressed, the family cars were outside. The family was downstairs. We joined them for a short family prayer. Leaving the house, one by one we stepped into the limousines. This trip would be the last time we would see Bob.*

After most of the people had left the house, only my parents and family were present.

Now, it was time to address the elephant in the room, beginning with funeral plans. Out of necessity, I called the funeral home and made arrangements for Bob's body to be picked up from the coroner. This set everything in motion. My pastor agreed the service and repass could be held at the church.

The evening quickly turned into night, and I was sleepy and drained. I just wanted to go to sleep. That night Ron stayed with us. The four of us cuddled together comforting one another.

The morning brought another set of stressful decisions to address. The undertaker called me to set up a meeting with him. He stated, "Bring the clothes you want us to dress your husband in for the viewing and funeral."

Deciding which suit to take was more than I could stand. Between the tears, a throbbing headache, and pleading prayers, I collected my emotions long enough to gather the necessary items. Ron escorted me to the funeral home and stayed with me through the meeting. My body was transiting from cold to hot. My palms were sweaty. My mouth was dry. The circulation in my legs were causing me to have painful cramps.

What I dreaded the most, time presented itself to me, there was one more transaction to complete. I had to pick out the casket. I wanted to scream as the undertaker showed us several different styles in the dimly lit room. The presentation didn't end there. Other casket options needed to be made regarding inside colors and design. I was ready to pass out. I had begun to feel lightheaded. The room felt like it was closing in on me. Finally, the undertaker escorted Ron and I back to his office.

The drive back home was quiet. Neither Ron nor I said anything. I wanted to crawl inside my purse and hide. That evening, so many people visited our home. Some genuinely expressing condolence, while others seem to come only for a good meal. The kids and I were introduced for the first time to some of Bob's family members.

The wake lasted into the wee hours of the morning. I needed to write the obituary, outline the program and have them delivered to the church by Friday. It was Wednesday, and I was still reeling from the movement of people coming and going to and from the house all day long. The rush of adrenaline throughout my body was running high. I did not have an appetite. I didn't have to look in the mirror to know that I had sagging bags underneath my eyes. I was truly operating under the power of the Holy Spirit. I was jumpy, wanting to run as fast as I could, without a specific destination.

My mind told me: *You are not going to make it.*

With all the faith I had in Jesus, Christ, I rebuked those thoughts, and said to myself, *I am an overcomer. I am victorious.*

I blamed myself for the sorrow my children and family were enduring because I could not absorb their pain. There wasn't anything I could possibly do to change the experience we were going through. The night before the funeral service I asked myself: *How did I get here?*

I promised myself after this ordeal, I would hold my precious children closer to my heart, move forward with the help of the Lord, and rebuild a life for us. With all my strength, I would protect them.

Saturday came like any other day of the week. I woke up drained. After the kids and I got dressed, the family cars were outside. The family was downstairs. We joined them for a short family prayer. Leaving the house, one by one we stepped into the limousines. This trip would be the last time we would see Bob.

Once at the church, the family was ushered into the sanctuary for the first viewing. Tears, tears, tears! I was so broken! My nerves jumped uncontrollably! My insides were crying out to God, "Please help me!"

What seemed like forever came to an end when the casket was closed. It was pre-arranged that the casket would be closed after the public viewing before the family marched in for the service. I felt the process of closing the casket while the family was there would have been too intense.

The family lined up in the church's foyer for the processional. The Pastor lead us in reciting the Lord's Prayer along with a passage of scripture:

**John 11:25**, "...I am the resurrection and the life; He that believeth in me, though he were dead, yet shall he live."

It was all I could do to keep my composure. Somehow, I escaped within myself to a quiet place. With Michael nestled on my right side, Michele nestled on the left side, we braved the service outline. So many thoughts were in and out of my recall. I had an eight-room house. It would be just the children and I.

I had so many questions.

*How would I be able to maintain this roof over our heads. What or who would I call if something needed to be fixed in the house? What plan did I have for the children getting off to school in the mornings?*

I started my day with the school district at seven o'clock a.m. The kids did not catch their bus until seven thirty o'clock a.m. At that time in the morning, it was still dark.

*Would they be able to securely lock up the house?*

I was breathing hard! While the service was continuing, I had to command my thoughts to a peaceful place, the calm of my faith resting in God. The instructions from the pulpit awakened me to the moment where the state of affairs were being conducted. The undertaker asked that the congregation remain seated until the body and the family left the sanctuary. The ride to the cemetery was grueling. To relieve some of the painful thoughts of my mind, I began counting houses as we passed them. Then the moment came when, the hearse, the family cars and all those who followed, turned into the gates of the cemetery. I realized this was the end! Bob's body would rest here until that great resurrection day. The cars pulled up to a chapel, where his body would be committed to the ground. The chapel served as an alternative to the customary standing around an open grave watching the casket being lowered into the ground. The Pastor echoed, "From ashes to ashes, dust to dust." The family each placed a rose on the casket and said good-by in their own way.

The ride back to the church was short. It looked like everyone was driving above the speed limit. No counting houses this time. So, I just gazed at the passing landscape. The repass fellowship was up-lifting with laughter, shared stories of Bob and tears that expressed he would no longer be part of future gatherings. I found enough strength as I spoke, thanking each and everyone who sacrificed to attend the funeral, comforted the family with their presence, the overwhelming food items brought to the house, the open door of the church the Pastor provided and the great cooks who supplied the incredible repass. I solicited prayers for our family as we mourn and heal.

I was so exhausted and ready to go home. My eyes were swollen and throbbing. I needed to rest!

## Chapter Twenty-Six: Thank You Jesus

*Marie's Prayer*

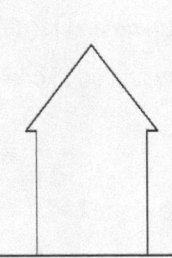

*Give me Paul's strength; I will have to survive on broken pieces. Lord, give me Mary's strength, to endure the death of a loved one. Lord give me favor to enter the upper room. Lord, please give me Abraham's strength; I too, am looking for a greater day.*

After the funeral, Ron took off the next week to be with us. I truly needed his support. I also took the entire week off from work. There were so many things that needed to be addressed. It was very difficult going back into the master bedroom. I felt the presence of death when I would enter the room. There was a spirit of coldness and sadness that trailed in the atmosphere. My thoughts were captured in bondage by the events that led up to his death. The images in my head were fresh as a spring morning in May. The recall of the children crying, shaking him, while his lifeless body remained unresponsive, resounded in my memory. I was grateful that Ron had cleaned up, after the death.

Day light hours gave me the strength to go to the bedroom. I managed to find important papers and get the necessary daily clothing needed. Under the bed we kept a fireproof strong box. The contents of the box housed our marriage license, house, and car insurance, etc. Also, there was a sheet of paper unfamiliar to me. When I opened it, it was in Bob's handwriting, outlining the family finances, debt, where to go to get the van inspected, who to call for emergencies, etc. I was so overwhelmed with emotions. I felt condemned by my feelings of anger towards him. Even in his hour of pain and suffering, he thought about me and the kids. He knew that verbally giving me this information would go in one ear and out the other.

I noticed his Bible on the nightstand located on his side of the bed. I remembered when the kids and I purchased that bible. We presented it to him, in church, the night he was ordained as an Elder. My first intention, regarding his Bible, was to place it in the casket with him. Then I thought about Michael. Perhaps someday he would cherish its memory. I had an inkling to open the Bible. I flipped through the Old and New Testament. Then, I began to examine the contents within the New Testament. I came across a scripture yellow highlighted zig-zag configuration that read:

*"The wife is bound by the law as long as her husband liveth; but if her husband be dead, she is at liberty to be married to whom she will; only in the Lord."*
**I Corinthians 7:39, KJV**

I continued to sit on the floor reading the scripture over and over; trying to process it all in the content in which his objective message would relate to my future. I believe he was trying to release me for a future marriage. It was an eerie feeling. Goose bumps rose on my arms. I wanted to throw the book across the room. Instead, I changed that tune. I thought not so, this is the Word of God. And I would act accordingly. I was NOT interested in another marriage! Although, my compassion was cordially grateful for his good-heartedness and love expressed toward me beyond the grave.

The outline of the family's financial picture did not fully reveal all debt. I was facing an up-hill battle, alone. At the end of the week, Ron hugged us, returning home to his family. The first night without him was rough, to say the least. It was difficult trying to get to sleep. I had so many aggravating, aggressive thoughts consuming my mind. I wasn't sure where to start in figuring out the sessions of need. I had no plan or vision. My instincts as a mother reminded me, I had two children who were depending on me. Everything about our situation seemed to be jumbled in a glass bottle.

I couldn't sleep in my bedroom, so I slept in the living room in Bob's favorite wing back chair. I did not realize how uncomfortable it was trying to rest in a chair position. I was hurting so bad from the pain of grief until a little discomfort seemed reasonable.

Somewhere between dusk and dawn, I was able to get a few hours of rest. The temperature outside had fallen ushering snowflakes. The house was cold. I rose to turn up the furnace and place the space heater in the bathroom so when the kids got up the house would be warm. I showered and dressed before I called them to get ready for school. This was the first day that we were on our own. This would be my proving ground of strength and endurance. I had reservations of doubt. As the minutes of the morning moved on, we managed to stay on schedule.

Before I left for work, I prayed and anointed them with blessed oil. I asked the Lord for protection and thanked Him for the Angels assigned to each one of us. The drive to work was painful. My thoughts were concerning about Michele and Michael leaving the house.

*Would they remember to put on the alarm? Would they remember to lock both the screen and outside doors?*

I was getting so worked up until I pulled over to the curb, for a couple of minutes to gain composure. Once at work, I called the school buildings where the kids were to receive confirmation that they had arrived safely.

Silently, I whispered, Thank you Jesus."

The pain of worry did not cease with morning confirmation. It rested until the end of day. I could feel stress revisit like the dawning of morning; it just comes. The kids would have to make it home two hours before my quitting time. I was praying that they had not misplaced or lost the house keys. I hoped they would remember the combinations of numbers to cut off the house alarm. My skin was breaking out even though, I had again started using Cortisone cream. Thoughts of them walking three blocks up the hill to the house was tearing me apart. It was difficult concentrating on my work assignments.

One morning when I was going to the mail room to get the mail for our office, the business manager was walking towards me. With a hardy, "Good morning," he then asked, "how are you and the kids doing?"

I thought, *what a welcome, wonderful question.*

His timing could not have been better. I acknowledged his greeting with a warm response. Then I gently expressed my concerns regarding Michele and Michael being latch key kids. He smiled and said, "You can have their bus changed to drop them off here at the Administration Building. They can go into the lunchroom, do their homework and watch television until it's time for you to leave at the end of the day."

I was so overjoyed! I must have thanked him several times over and over. The Lord heard my cry, provided a way for us, giving me favor with the School District's Business Manager. For the rest of the day, I was singing gospel hymns of joy and giving thanks!

Going into the second month after Bob's death, I was still sleeping in the wing back chair. I was constantly in prayer for guidance and strength. I didn't sleep sound due to fear. I could always here creaking, wind whistling, and voices outside. Previously, I had an alarm system put in the house. The system covered all the exterior doors but not the windows. To have the latter included, the monthly payment exceeded my financial range. So, the kids and I went to the local hardware store and purchased rod iron window gates for the family room windows. The low windows in the dining room and kitchen were glass block, as well as the basement windows. Glass block windows provided an element of security. I didn't have the correct tools to place the window grates on the outside of the windows, so I screwed them on the inside of the windows. It took a while to secure them. Once confident of their placement, I drew back the curtains. Things looked great! I was proud of myself!

The next weekend the kids and I decided to get a guard dog. The following Saturday, we went to the Animal Rescue League to find a watch dog that would fit with our family. This was a new experience for me. I didn't grow up with a dog. I had no idea how to care for a dog. Yet, I was just as excited as the kids, with reservations. My concerns included: where the dog would sleep, would the kids walk and feed the dog, and how would the dog react when left alone. With all these thoughts and more, I took a deep breath and proceeded with my plan.

Once at the Animal Rescue League, I was asked a series of questions. My answers would help build a profile for a comparable fit. After getting answers to my questions, we were escorted into a private room. Soon after, they brought several breeds of dogs. None seemed to fit our family's dynamics. Then they brought in Buffy. She was a female mix of a Golden Retriever and German Sheppard. Immediately, the kids took to her and she to them. I wasn't on board, but I was trying. That afternoon, Buffy came home with us. She was a great guard dog! She would let you know if anyone was approaching the house. Buffy and I had an agreement, she would sit beside me without jumping on me. It was the kids that played with her, fed her, and bathed her. She lived until Michael turned eighteen.

While at church attending evening service, I got a phone call from Michael. Buffy had strangled herself. From the chair on the back porch, Buffy jumped down and her chained wrapped around the arm of the chair, strangling her. We mourned her. Her death allowed me to realize how much of a family member she had been.

The Lord extended His grace as He guided us through the spring and summer months. I was still sleeping in the wingback chair asking God to help me keep my thoughts focused on the tapestry of concerns for which I was responsible. My daily prayer requested the Lord to let me live, through His guidance and strength to raise Michele and Michael to adulthood. I wanted to experience their maturity.

*Give me Paul's strength; I will have to survive on broken pieces. Lord, give me Mary's strength, to endure the death of a loved one. Lord give me favor to enter the upper room. Lord, please give me Abraham's strength; I too, am looking for a greater day.*

One morning while sitting at my work desk during my morning prayer and still in a moment of thanksgiving, the Lord impressed upon me the phrase, "My Time." There was nothing more revealed. Several days later, as I continued to weigh the significance of the phrase, the Lord spoke again and repeated, "My Time."

Fall debuted the city with extreme coldness. I felt it was too early to turn on the furnace, so I continued to use both electric heaters. The kitchen was the coldest. I needed a new kitchen floor. The flooring was linoleum, but it had two tears. One tear at the back door and the second tear by the kitchen sink. Previously, my aunt introduced me to a handy man (Charles). I called him with my concerns. He agreed to give me a quote. When he got to the house, he took note of the flooring situation. He then asked, "Can I look at the joists underneath this floor?"

I said, "Yes." And directed him to the basement where they were located. When Charles came upstairs and entered back into the kitchen, he had a look on his face that didn't look promising. He gently gave me the disturbing news.

"There are eight layers of flooring resting on the joists, which is causing the floor to buckle."

Immediately, I saw dollar signs, my heart began to beat faster. I braced myself for additional bad news.

Charles explained, "To do the job effectively, I would need to pull not only the current flooring, but the seven other layers beneath."

What he said next took me by surprise.

"I will just charge you one hundred dollars to pull the old flooring up and replace it with tile, if you supply the materials."

I unleashed a resounding, "Yes." I was so relieved! I knew the Lord touched his heart in his decision regarding the floor due to the price he quoted. Little did I know then, this would not be the last time we would enter into a contractual agreement. I needed other work done on the house as well.

After the tile was laid, Charles asked, "Does your kitchen always stay cold?"

I answered, "Yes."

He responded, "That is because there is no insulation in the walls. If you look in between the opening between the kitchen wall and the back door, you can see what I am saying."

I looked and verified what he was saying. I almost fainted when he described the process to insulate. There were two choices: blown in insulation or gutting the kitchen walls. Insulate or replace the walls? I decided to wait until later. At that time, it wasn't a high priority.

I thought, *it would lower my high gas bills.*

Charles said, "Call me when you are ready."

*Marie Jenkins', My Time*

# Chapter Twenty-Seven: Widowhood

*He Is Here with Me*

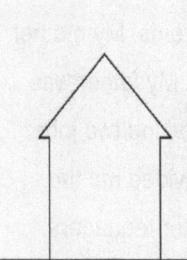

*I climbed hills, tunneled through mountains, got stuck in the valley and survived rough terrain and puddle through dark spaces. But I held on to the hope that someday I would reach the light at the end of the tunnel. The Lord promised through His Word that He would never leave me. So, I held tight to His unchanging hands.*

I will digress and insert my appointment here. The year prior to my husband's death, I was appointed District Missionary by the State Mother of Western Pennsylvania, Jurisdiction. This appointment included the supervision of women within the five churches in our District. I joined the rank of experienced District Missionaries who did not warmly welcome me. We were all members of the State Mother's cabinet, which carried a whole new set of required responsibilities. My appointment fostered resentment from other women in the church who believed they should have been chosen.

This caused me pain and discomfort. Some felt I was too young for the position, while others coveted it. When the death of my husband occurred, their compassion was non-existent. I couldn't grieve. I was earnestly trying to keep my head above water and life from spiraling out of control. I was experiencing pressures from all sides, church family and members of my family.

I was in the development of church leadership along with wearing several hats of servitude. I was an actively involved mother with the children. I became a caregiver to both of my aging parents. My mother was disabled, needing the assistance of a wheelchair. My father was experiencing the beginning stages of senility. I was working two jobs: one full-time, one part-time. The part-time position provided me the opportunity to supervise Michele, Michael and four other teenagers. Determined to better my life, I enrolled in higher education. I cared nine credits a semester as I exercised and maintained my responsibilities.

Some days were more over whelming than others. Some days I told myself I couldn't do another thing. Some days, I did not even know what to pray or how to pray for it. I was in so much emotional pain. I felt like Dorothy in the Wiz, spinning in the tornado. The stress of Bob's death alone caused trauma to my body. It took me into early menopause. Despite my efforts of care, my skin continued to have periods of breakout. My eye lids twitched day and night. It felt like bugs crawling under my skin and I couldn't sleep at night. I was a mess!

Yet, I kept going forward, holding on to the strength of God. It was His amazing grace that covered me! Some nights I would cry until my eyes wouldn't open, from the swelling. However, I did not miss a day of living or giving God praise! The Lord did grant me some good days, where I could exhale. I climbed hills, tunneled through mountains, got stuck in the valley and survived rough terrain and puddle through dark spaces. But I held on to the hope that someday I would reach the light at the end of the tunnel. The Lord promised through His Word that He would never leave me. So, I held tight to His unchanging hands.

A mother alone raising children often assumes both roles, mother, and father. One day the Lord spoke to my heart and said, "If you trust and obey me, I will help you raise your children. I created you to be a woman, one role, a mother." I received His Word.

It was difficult when I prayed to include all those who had and were still mistreating me. I remember repeating through my prayers over and over, I loved them, Lord. At first, I was not sincere, nor could I feel any love for them. I was still angry. In fact, I didn't want to love them!

My thoughts were telling me, *you are wasting your time.*

Yet, I continued night after night to pray for those who willfully despised me, making my life a living hell.

I can't really give a specific day or time when the change occurred. But I do remember when I was in the company of those who had mistreated me and realizing they no longer held a stronghold over me! There was nothing tugging at my heart, nor did I have evil thoughts toward them. Alas, I was delivered from unforgiveness. I could speak to them in confidence, knowing the Lord had empowered me to love my enemies! I was making progress. They were baby steps, but I was moving forward.

There were other giants and battles. Standing in the obedience to the Lord, I had His assurance, He would fight on my behalf.

My plate was full, and I did not have time to get constipated.

Several months after the first year of Bob's death, one night I was sitting in the wing back chair praying. The encounter was as if the Lord was holding me in His bosom as He spoke to my heart, "Why do you fear? He is with me."

The Lord was referring to Bob. At that moment, I closed prayer, went upstairs, and slept in my bed. The weekend that followed, I cleaned out his closet. I called the head of the Elders' Board and asked him if some of the Elders or Ministers could fit Bob's suits.

The next day the Chairman of the Board of Elders came and thanked me for my generosity.

Slowly, I began to settle into widowhood.

# Chapter Twenty-Eight: Normalcy

*God Protects and Provides*

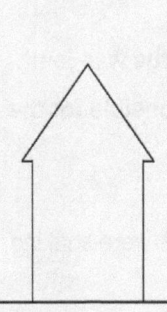

> *I had cried so much until my tear ducts were dry. My eyes were swollen. My skin was irritated and sore. My head was throbbing. By this time the kids were also crying and asking me what was wrong. I tried to give them the best answer I could. I told them not to worry. I tried to reassure them, that things would work out. I did not have the strength to think about a solution. My pain consumed me.*

It was tax time and federal and state taxes needed to be filed. I gathered the documents needed and began to follow the filing instructions online. I checked the box indicating my status, widow. As the information from the documents were inputted, I noticed the gradual calculations did not reflect a refund. I thought perhaps I had made an error. Regardless, I submitted the return and waited on the I.R.S. to respond.

After four weeks of waiting, I received a letter from the I.R.S. stating I owed the government over ten thousand dollars. I re-read the letter. The verbiage did not change. I felt my heart racing. A blunt pain entered my head causing it to throb. My eyes were getting glassy. I felt warm and sweaty. Again, I re-read the letter. It still read the same way. I convinced myself, surly, they had made a mistake. I wrote a response asking for a re-calculation. I also included a copy of Bob's death certificate.

In about two weeks I received the second correspondence from the I.R.S. Department of the Treasury stating:

**When your previous taxes were filed, the filing status was joint. This included you. Therefore, you are legally responsible for the debt.**

When I read those words, I couldn't breathe. My hands were shaking, my mouth became dry. My insides felt like Jell-o.

*I don't have this kind of money.* I thought to myself.

Terrible thoughts were entering into my head.

*What if I cannot pay. What would be my demise? Would they require me to do jail time? I have children! What would be my appeal?*

I began to cry. I was so afraid. Further down in the letter there was clause suggesting a payment plan, but only to their financial discretion. None of their options were financially conducive for me. Just when I could see the shore peaking over the horizon, now this - a wave of great magnitude pulling me back under. I was clinging with all my strength to my faith. Before I responded to the letter, I prayed and asked God to guide me.

(When my husband retired, he had a security business. The income from the business was the reason for the ten thousand dollars back payment.)

I called the I.R.S. explaining my situation. The agent on the phone was very compassionate. He said, "I will approve payment to be taken from future tax returns until the balance is paid. Interest will still accrue. If you send in additional money it will help."

I felt relief. I thanked the agent. I thanked the Lord. I was disappointed because I was depending on yearly refunds to assist with the upgrades for the house projects. After the conversation with the I.R.S. I rested my head. It was heavy and hurting.

Winter arrived on time. It was December 23rd and snow covered the ground and our tree branches. The snow rested between the opening in the fence. The car was buried resembling a silhouette. The landscape was picturesque and beautiful. It looked like a winter wonderland. The scenery was blue-ribbon worthy. Each snowflake was distinguished in shape and size. Some set poised and pretty.

That evening I was preparing food for our Christmas dinner. I asked the kids to take their laundry baskets to the laundry room, in the basement, and wash their clothes. Unbeknown to me, the washing machine was not completely wringing the water out of the clothes. Instead of informing me, they placed the clothes dripping with water into the dryer. The extra water in the clothes burned out the hot element in the dryer.

In the meantime, while I was cooking and baking, suddenly the stove went out. My first thought was it might have been a circuit malfunction. I went to the basement to check the circuit box. All the circuit breakers were on. This is when I also learned about the condition of the washer and dryer. At that moment I was more concerned about the stove. I returned to the kitchen. I immediately turned off the stove. I waited a few minutes, before I tried again to turn on the stove. The results were not positive. I was frantic!

I began crying, "Why? Why? Why? Lord, I can't take much more."

I realized for weeks the freezer was collecting ice although it was frost free. It was getting old, but still worked. I felt if it was working, it didn't need to be fixed right away. I was so overwhelmed, I ended up on the kitchen floor in a fetal position, asking God again, "Why?"

I had cried so much until my tear ducts were dry. My eyes were swollen. My skin was irritated and sore. My head was throbbing. By this time the kids were also crying and asking me what was wrong. I tried to give them the best answer I could. I told them not to worry. I tried to reassure them, that things would work out. I did not have the strength to think about a solution. My pain consumed me.

Fortunately, one of the members of my church had previously invited us to have Christmas dinner with her family. I called her to make sure my R.S.V.P. was still valid. She confirmed that it was. I thanked her and shared with her my dilemma.

Christmas day, I remember lying on her couch for most of the evening. I was so broken, embarrassed, and helpless. I was reminded when the Lord provided a ram in the bush. With this I was comforted. I didn't have an appetite. Sister Wilson packed food for us to take home. I thanked her for her kindness, hospitality, and love. She saved Christmas for us.

The Monday after Christmas, I went to the store that sold scratch and dent appliances. I purchased a new electric stove, frost free refrigerator, washer, dryer, and a big screen television for the family room. Along with the appliances being purchased, I included a five-year warranty. The following Saturday the appliances were scheduled to be delivered.

*What else could possibly go wrong?*

I would soon find out.

The old washer and dryer could not be removed. The door-jam leading into the laundry room was too small for the removal of the old appliances or for the entry of the new ones.

When my Bob was working on the basement, he divided the laundry room with a doorway. Unfortunately, the doorway did not allow exit or entry. The doorway had to be removed. The installers did not do any carpentry work.

If that was not enough, the stove installer, an older man, was able to remove my old electric stove. However, once that was done, he said with tobacco in his gums, "Ms. I can't hook up your stove. You have a one ten line coming from the outside breaker box into your kitchen. The new stove requires a two twenty connecting line. You sure are lucky, your house could have blown up, cause the old stove required the same two twenty connecting lines."

I almost passed out! My thoughts were all over the place and my head was spinning with pain. Again, I was thanking God for His divine protection! When I did gain control of my thoughts, I called Charles. I explained the situation. Then I ask if he could help me. I needed to have the stove connected, immediately.

He said, "I will be there in the morning. I will bring with me a friend who is a registered electrician." He further stated, "You can take care of the cost of his labor later. We will get you connected first."

I thanked him.

Early the next morning, they both came and connected the stove. A complete week had passed. The washing machine and dryer sat in the basement without being installed. For the first time in years, the kids and I went to the neighborhood laundry mat. They thought it was cool. In fact, they had a good time rolling the carts around and taking turns putting and taking out the clothes.

One evening I was venting to my girlfriend regarding the occurrences involving the washer and dryer. After she prayed with me, she said, "I have a friend, who is a retired Electrician. Tomorrow I will ask him to look at your washer and dryer."

I was so relieved and hopeful.

Saturday morning, they both came to the house. Brenda sat with me as we had conversations over a cup of tea for her and a cup of coffee for me. Mr. Bennett went to the basement. Hours later he immerged proclaiming, "The job is complete. Your washer and dryer are connected."

Tears of joy streamed down my face. Before I could ask him about his charge. He volunteered, "Ms. there is no charge. Just remember me in your prayers."

I couldn't resist. I threw my arms around his neck and said, "You will be included in all my daily prayers."

Finally, some normalcy had been reestablished.

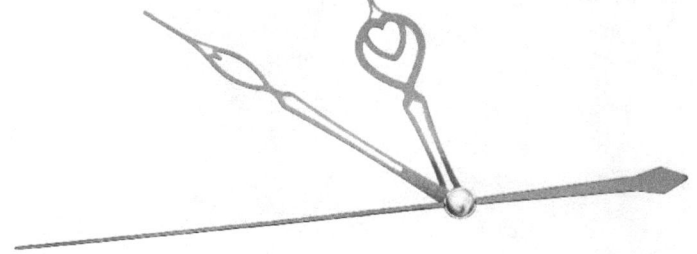

*Marie Jenkins', My Time*

# Chapter Twenty-Nine: The Wings of Christ
From Labor to Rest

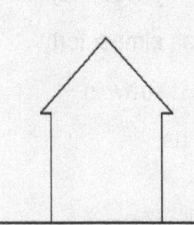

> I had reached the point where I felt blessed to be able to accomplish the responsibilities I had. My day would begin at five o'clock in the morning and often end at eleven or eleven thirty at night. I realized I was being carried on the wings of Christ.

The health of my parents was taking a turn for the worst. With the unanimous discussion of my brothers, myself, the children, and parents, we relocated them closer to us, in Pittsburgh. They were now within a ten-minute drive. My father had difficulty adjusting. He wanted to stay and continue to Pastor the church. Before leaving, my dad was honored with Emeritus. Over and over, we explained to my dad the dangers he and mom faced living thirty miles from us. Prior to relocating our parents to Pittsburgh, numerous times, Dad would leave the house driving, become confused and got lost. This caused pain and worry to my mother, and with us too. It had become constant, I would receive wee hour morning phone calls from Mom stating, "I do not know where your father is. He left the house this morning, going to the Senior Citizen Center. He has been gone for hours."

One very profound incident comes to mind. One Thursday evening, my dad left Burgettstown on his way to Pittsburgh to hear me preach. He never made it. I thought he didn't make it because he didn't have anyone that would ride with him. I later found out, he got confused, made a wrong turn, and was on his way to New York. My brothers, Ron and I devised an all-out search for Dad/Grandpa. It was almost forty-eight hours before he reemerged. That became the last straw in determining our decision to move them both closer to us.

Everyone was on board knowing the responsibility of becoming caregivers. We all took turns with their care. My brothers were so sub servant to their needs. Ron along with the grandchildren would drive from Columbia Maryland to assist and visit. Michele and Michael attended to them several days a week. Mom and dad were being spoiled! And they were enjoying it. They both resembled the picture of health, while we were dragging from exhaustion. However, it was so much easier navigating their care.

Weekends had become a joyous time. The family would gather with great conversations and good food. No question, our destination on the weekend was with Mom and Dad, Grandma, and Grandpa's place. Some watched television, while others played chess and checkers. Dad won most games. He was in his glory. I didn't know if they let him win or just lost. From my perspective, it looked like they were trying their best to beat him. I would cook enough for Mom and Dad to have leftovers throughout the week. There was always enough food for the family to break bread while we were together.

*Marie Jenkins', My Time*

In the meantime, I was also completing my degree at Carlow University. I was still working two jobs, ministering full time, raising two children, and caring for my parents. The demands were great and all important. I wore numerous hats: motherhood, caretaker, Evangelist (District Missionary), employee. I was beginning to experience the wear and tear on my body. I had reached the point where I felt blessed to be able to accomplish the responsibilities I had. My day would begin at five o'clock in the morning and often end at eleven or eleven thirty at night. I realized I was being carried on the wings of Christ.

After a few enjoyable years with our parents, the Lord called my father from labor to rest. It was very painful for us, especially my mother. They had been married over fifty years. The patriarch of the family was no longer with us. The void was unbearable. We had him all our lives. But the Lord needed him more. It was time for his reward and rest. Challenged with the task to begin funeral preparations, I needed the input of the family and the desires of my mother. With assistance from the Adjutancy Core of our church my mother and family, I planned the home going service for my father.

Not long after the celebration of my father's life, my mother's health began to deteriorate, rapidly. With her declining health, she needed twenty-four-hour care. We found her the best nursing home available. To our satisfaction, my mother had a private room and bathroom. There were sconces on the wall. Per our request, her room was painted in her favorite color, light green. Her clothes were hung in an armoire and beside her bed was a nightstand with family pictures digitally displayed.

*Marie Jenkins', My Time*

My brothers purchased her a sixty-inch television and had it mounted on the wall. They also purchased her a small refrigerator. It was stocked with her favorite snacks and drinks. The personal care gave her continued contact with each family member. On the days I didn't have class, I would pick up the kids after school, grab a pizza and wings, with destination Mom. The evenings I did have class, I would make her my last stop of the day. The most difficult times to visit were winter months. I didn't fear snow on the roads but was petrified by black ice.

# Chapter Thirty: A Good and Faithful Servant

*A Sovereign God*

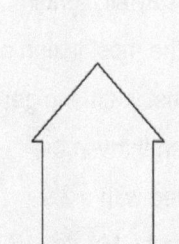

> *I carried the burden of guilt for my children. The death of their father caused so much pain. I wish I could have carried their pain, as well. I know God is sovereign. And His will is perfect. He moves on time, in His own time. I never accused God of our suffering. I accepted His will, even when I did not understand.*

The University I attended, sat on a hill (like most of Pittsburgh). Night school parking was challenging. Most evenings I was forced to park in the upper lots. These lots were located three to four blocks from the main campus. When blizzard winds blew, they would take away my breath. The coldness from the winds pierced through my winter layering, chilling me to the bone. Security patrolled the lots. But sometimes there were no signs of them. That's when fear would grip me.

My first class started about an hour after my arrival. This gave me time to eat in the student cafeteria. After eating, it was hard keeping my eyes open. I would drift off into sleep. Out of kindness, fellow students would wake me so I would not be late for class. Getting to class was another journey. I had to climb three flights of concrete steps just to reach the building where classes were held. Once in the building, there was another two flights of stairs to reach the second floor. With all that walking, I retained my girly figure. I developed strong leg muscles, as well. Some nights I would get severe leg cramps in my calf muscles due to the long hours of walking.

When I had large typing project assignments, I would stay all night in the school's computer room. The week of finals were the most taxing on my mind and body. I would leave the computer room just in time to get home, shower, change clothes and be at work by seven thirty in the morning. My testimony: the struggle paid off, I graduated with a 3.9 average. I am an inductee into the National Honor Society. My accomplishments were made possible because of Christ. He strengthened me to finish my course. At the end of my senior year, a letter of graduation confirmation was sent. One very special sentence stands out to me, it states:

**You have met all Carlow University requirements for graduation.**

Each time I read it, it is a reminder of the toll, sacrifice, hard work and prayers that enabled me to achieve my desire. Notwithstanding, I someday want to hear the voice of Lord say, "Welcome my good and faithful servant, enter into the Kingdom of God."

I was adamant regarding annual health check-ups for the kids. Complying with the scheduled appointment, after work I picked up the kids for their appointment with the Pediatrician. After the appointment was over, we headed back to the van only to find, I had a flat front tire. I had already had a nerve wrenching day at work. I was tired, hungry, and cold. I was weary and out done! I called for a mechanic through my car club membership. We waited in the van. Within about twenty minutes the mechanic pulled up. He began to change the tire. I got out the van to speak with him. I was not ready for the news he gave.

He said, "Ma'am, your inspection sticker is out of compliance, your van tag is six months old, and you have no back breaks."

I felt a blood rush shoot straight to my head! I leaned on the van to gain composure. I stood there long after the mechanic left. At that moment I did not feel the blustery coldness of the night. I was having a conversation with God, thanking him for protection. Being drained, I let Him know, "Lord, I can't take much more. I am being stretched beyond my endurance levels.," I whispered silently, "please help me, God."

When my husband lived, he took care of the vehicles. I had been spoiled by his due diligence. I was in uncharted areas. Moving forward in the days to come, I took care of everything the mechanic suggested. When I stopped and thought of the miles I had traveled over roads and hills in Pittsburgh without back brakes, I broke out in a hallelujah praise. Chills came over me. So many dreadful things could have happened, but God!

Michele was in twelfth grade, ready to graduate from high school. I was a proud mama. I couldn't go to my prom. But I made sure Michele would go to hers, in style. She was a beautiful date, draped in a body fitting lemon yellow gown. Grandma gifted her gown for her graduation present. Watching Michele grow gave me great everlasting memories. She was concluding a huge milestone. She gave me the chance to experience what it would have been like if I would have attended my prom. I celebrated her as if it had been me.

The end of summer put us on the road traveling to her first semester of higher education. Two years later, Michael, my sunshine and youngest, graduated from high school. Again, I was a proud mama. His life had not been scared by drugs, felonies, or fatherhood. When I witnessed him walk across the stage to receive his diploma, I reflected in a moment of thought, his manhood. By faith God brought our family to promise. When the diploma was placed in his hands, I gave thanksgiving to our Lord and Savior, Jesus Christ. Michael won; he beat the odds. Victory fit well on him.

Grandma gifted Michael with professional graduation pictures. Michael went to his prom exuding the presence of a prince. He was in his moment. Good success was his forward fortune.

God answered my prayers. All three of my children were young adults. The Lord moved the bar forward in my direction. I would be celebrating the same joys that I witnessed from their lives. Within the next few months, I would be graduating. I had previously obtained an Associate Degree in Business. For a few minutes I looked back over my life, remembering the distance of our arrival to this point.

We endured rough times, times of sorrow, scarce times of hopelessness, but not without or forgetting good times. I was grateful for the people placed in my life, who stood with me through it all. I was at a milestone.

There were possibilities waiting for me to achieve. My dreams had not fallen. I didn't have any expectation of marrying. I could finally concentrate on me.

I carried the burden of guilt for my children. The death of their father caused so much pain. I wish I could have carried their pain, as well. I know God is sovereign. And His will is perfect. He moves on time, in His own time. I never accused God of our suffering. I accepted His will, even when I did not understand.

Prayerfully, the children and I can move forward. A prosperous future awaits us.

When I purchased my cap and gown, I showed them to my mother. There were tears in her eyes as she said, "I am so proud of you. You have raised your children and now you can pursue your dreams."

By this time, I was crying as well. I thanked her for encouragement, words of wisdom, being a great, real woman of God, helping me financially, and just being my mom.

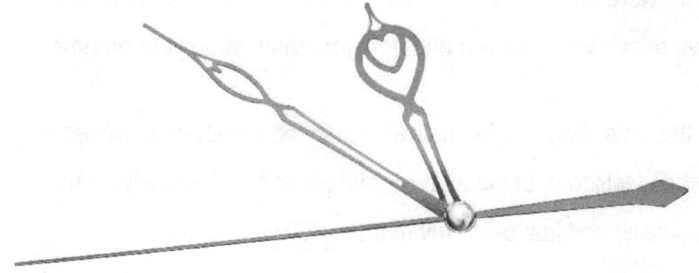

*Marie Jenkins', My Time*

# Chapter Thirty-One: Love Is in The Air

*Weak In The Knees*

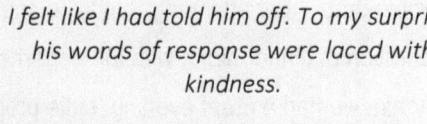

*I felt like I had told him off. To my surprise, his words of response were laced with kindness.*

*He said, "I will. I have already asked the Lord for His angles to cover you. Speak to you soon."*

*I felt like a heel! Yet, at that moment, I was confident, he was the one!*

After the retirement of a close dear friend, she and her husband relocated to Florida. Once settled into their new residence, I was invited to spend the 2010 Christmas holiday with them and have dinner with their brother-n-law, who was a widower. Sorrowfully, I declined the first invitation. Keeping in touch, once again they extended the first invitation. The second request I conferred with my children. Surprisingly, they all said I should go.

Twice before, the children sent me to our church's National Convention in St. Louis. An all-expense paid trip, hoping I would meet someone who would be looking for a wife. Well, it didn't happen, but I enjoyed both trips.

I agreed to the invitation. While in flight, I was anticipating a pleasurable stay in Florida. Saturday evening the four of us had dinner. I had a wonderful evening despite the absence of bells or whistles. I noticed Mr. Maurice was looking at me all evening. When I would look towards him, his eyes would drop. After attending Sunday's church service, I assisted in the preparation of dinner along with the eagerness to see Mr. Maurice. Again, we had a great evening. Little progress between Mr. Jenkins and I ensued. Following dinner and a movie, Mr. Jenkins informed us he was leaving. As he moved towards the door, I waved good-bye from the love seat. I was quite upset that he did not ask me to walk him to the door. Nor did he give me a good-night salutation. Truly, he was unaware of who I was!

Monday arrived and I was unaware that this day would change my life and that the miracle of a love story would begin to evolve. That afternoon my friends took me to the Orlando airport, prayed for me and with me, and wished me a safe trip home. I was informed by the airline, that the connecting flight in Chicago was cancelled due to inclement weather. I was resolved to spend the night at the airport and catch a non-stop flight the next morning. I would still make it to work on time. Several hours passed when I received a phone call from my friend asking how the progress of my travel was occurring. I tried to conceal my location not to inconvenience them. She became suspicious and asked, "Where are you now?"

I continued to be evasive, expressing my appreciation for their southern hospitality. My pretense was given away by the enormous noise from the water fountain in the background. As the conversation concluded, my friends were on their way to pick me up. They did not want me to spend the night in the airport.

In the meantime, I received a phone call from Mr. Jenkins. (*My phone number had been given to Mr. Jenkins by his sister-n-law at the same time when her and her husband were coming to the airport to pick me up.*) When I answered, a soft, gentle, Barry White voice said, "Having a little difficulty. You could have called me; I would have picked you up."

I was stunned. I kept looking at the phone in disbelief.

I thought, *I spent a weekend here in Florida and you didn't say ten words to me. Now, you want to talk.*

I didn't know whether to be insulted or flattered.

I responded with sarcasm, "Thank you for your concern."

He further stated, "When you get home, please call me. I want to make sure you arrived safely."

I was more infuriated than the first time. With the same sarcastic pitch in my voice, I said, "I will give you the arrival time. When you think I am home, you can call me."

It felt so good speaking those words. I felt like I had told him off. To my surprise, his words of response were laced with kindness.

He said, "I will. I have already asked the Lord for His angles to cover you. Speak to you soon."

I felt like a heel! Yet, at that moment, I was confident, he was the one!

From this point, a friendship developed. At the end of the day, after arriving back home, I got a phone call from Mr. Maurice. This time I was receptive. We had a good conversation. He was charming! I was getting weak at the knees.

Twice a week I looked forward to receiving a call from Mr. Maurice. Knowing he might call; I had started carrying my cell phone with me. I was hooked, like a junkie. We discussed everything from how the earth orbits to how God's Word works. He was interesting to talk to. We were on first name bases by this time, along with special ring tones attached to our names. I began to receive beautiful red and yellow roses, balloons, gourmet food trays, jewelry, a fruit basket, and specialty cupcakes.

Valentine Day, Maurice sent me a singing telegram at my job, along with a half dozen balloons. The man was in a top hat and tails. He sang the poem Maurice composed:

Marie Jenkins', My Time

Happy Valentine's Day Marie
Valentine's Day is for lovers
Love is sure in the air
Merci, I can't wait to see your face
For no other woman compares
First date is up and coming
January is so, so far away
I guess I'll have to settle for
A telegram to tell you
All the sweet things I'd like to say.
Valentine, I sure am thankful
For our friends
What a dinner that turned out to be
And now just look where we're at
Florida would be much brighter
With your smile by my side
Oh, I almost forgot to say
When I come in January
I'm taking you on a magic carpet ride.

*Marie Jenkins', My Time*

# Chapter Thirty-Two: Your Blessing

*Ceremonies and Confirmations*

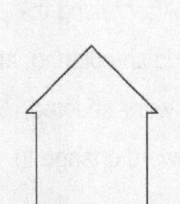

*"You are fearful with making a decision regarding retirement. Be not afraid, the Lord has spoken regarding your situation. You are standing in your blessing! You can rest on His Words. Be at peace and go forward."*

As the months moved, I was preparing for graduation. When the month of May arrived, I was excited to walk across the stage, receive my degree, turn my tassel, and share the moment with the children, family, friends and Maurice. He could not physically attend. I had his well wishes and blessings. The ceremony would be taped for my mother. This was the first step into a better future.

The day of the graduation ceremony, Michele was washing my hair, when we heard the doorbell ring. We asked each other, "Who is that?"

My head was still under the faucet. Michele opened the door and screamed. I got a towel and turned to see what was wrong. All I could see were a cluster of balloons. At first, I thought maybe I was seeing soap bubbles, when Michele belted out, "Mr. Maurice sent you balloons to celebrate your graduation day."

I was moved to tears. I called and thanked him over and over. A couple days before graduation, I made an appointment with my Primary Care doctor. I was feeling anxious. There were so many things happening at once. The evidence showed on my skin. The doctor gave me a prescription to calm my nerves and clear up my skin. After taking the medicine, I felt worse. My legs were swollen with a reddish coloring, and they throbbed continually. By the second day my feet were affected, also. At the time I did not contribute the sudden downward change to the medicine.

Needless, to say, the night of graduation, I was in so much pain. Michael had to help me walk to the auditorium where the graduation celebration was to take place. The distance was not overwhelmingly long, but because of the pain in my legs and feet it seemed like a country mile. My son had to hold me up as I took each painful step to reach the entrance of the Soldiers and Sailor Memorial Hall.

I was praying that I could get through the ceremony. When my name was called, I was in excruciating pain. With my head up high, a smile and a wave, I proudly strolled across the stage, receiving my well-earned reward, Bachelor of Art Degree in Social Work. I had taken two pain killers to be able to meet afterwards with the family for a late dinner.

In a couple of weeks, the school district would end the school year and open in June with a new fiscal year. If I wanted to retire, I would have to submit the paperwork by June first. For the remaining weeks in May, I was sitting on pins and needles regarding my decision. I did not have a specific plan relating to my future employment. But I felt the unction of the Lord comforting me. I just needed to launch out on faith.

The last Sunday in May is when I received confirmation from the Lord regarding the decision of retirement.

Our church had a guest afternoon speaker. While he was engaged delivering the Word of God, he stopped and asked me to come to the altar. Likewise, he called his mother to stand beside me. I was so embarrassed. Little did I know what was coming in my favor. The preacher asked for his mother to place her hand on my stomach. He began to pray. Afterwards he said, "You are fearful with making a decision regarding retirement. Be not afraid, the Lord has spoken regarding your situation. You are standing in your blessing! You can rest on His Words. Be at peace and go forward."

I gave the Lord my best praise!

Monday morning, I submitted paperwork to the school district for my retirement. This was one of my best decisions, ever. I never looked back with regret. When I retired, I did not have any irons in the fire.

My thoughts were, *should I continue the next level in education or pursue a new career?*

Well, a new career was eminent. I was invited to a church affiliated banquet. I was enjoying the food and the fellowship. At the buffet table I ran into Debra. She was the Director of Service Coordination. Through conversation she mentioned, she happened to see my Resume from a position I applied for within her organization. She commented, "You are too qualified for that position you applied for. I am developing a position that will assist me in daily operations." She went on to say, "You are a good fit for mine."

Weeks later, I was called in for an interview with the Director of Service Coordination. One of her Supervisors interviewed me for the position as Debra monitored my responses to various questions.

Once confirmed, I assisted Debra in finishing the job description as she opened up the conversation to include my preferences, full time or part time?

*Who does that?*

What a great opportunity, given. I started with a part-time schedule. And worked my way up finally to full-time.

*Marie Jenkins', My Time*

# Chapter Thirty-Three: My Kind of Man

*Birthdays and Bliss*

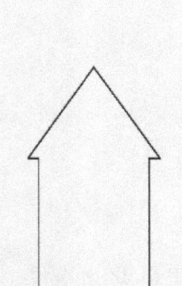

*We were escorted to a booth where the ring was examined under a microscope and was given visual and verbal certification. Maurice removed himself to take care of the finances. As I sat waiting for his return, he stepped back into the booth, kneeled on one knee in front of me, recited a speech, and asked, "Will you marry me?"*

When I would visit my mom, I would keep her up to date on the progress between Maurice and I. Six months passed and plans were being developed for his trip to Pittsburgh for our first date. This event would occur on my birthday, January 21st of the following year.

Each day knitted our hearts closer. Each night we took turns praying together.

January approached with mounting excitement.

Maurice suggested I pick out the finest restaurant in Pittsburgh for dinner and include a cultural event as well.

Finally, my birthday arrived.

That morning I received a dozen red roses with a note:

**Happy Birthday, I will see you soon.**

I was excited and nervous at the same time. I tried on dress after dress making sure my choice was right for the occasion.

Maurice phoned:

"I am here in Pittsburgh, Happy Birthday."

And I never stopped smiling. There was pandemonium in the house. Michael was on his way to escort Maurice from the hotel to the house. Meanwhile, Michele was trying to help me get dressed.

Michael called with excitement in his voice, "We are on our way," while asking Michele, "is mom ready?"

I remained cool as a cucumber, while simultaneously shaking in my shoes. Once Maurice arrived at the house the kids and friends greeted him. They did a thorough investigation.

With one foot in front of the other, I glided down the staircase to meet the one I had waited for. I liked what I saw! He looked so much better the second time! He greeted me with a warm, million-dollar smile, a holy birthday kiss and tender embrace. After spending time with the kids and friends, we were on our way to dinner.

The Cadillac he rented seemed to glide across the roads. I really did feel like I was on a carpet ride. The view of Pittsburgh from the top of Mt. Washington at night was spectacular. This dinner had bells and whistles!

After dinner we attended a musical at the August Wilson Cultural Center.

Later, when Maurice met my mother, there was an instant connection. She shared with me, "That's your husband." She too, began receiving gifts and cards.

Some evenings when I would visit my mother, I would video call Maurice where he and my mother could see each other when they talked. She loved it. He showed her his office and the board room where he had leadership conferences.

Over the next eleven months, I experienced an exciting courtship. We attended special events together. Maurice was invited to attend my family reunion. They fell in love with him, agreeing with my mother that he was the one. My children and grandchildren vacationed in Florida, meeting his children and grandchildren. Maurice introduced me to his Pastor and church family.

Thanksgiving 2012 sealed our relationship.

Maurice was invited to Columbia Maryland, by my eldest son, to spend the holiday weekend in his home along with our family. This would be the first time Ron would meet Maurice.

"Do you have a Steeler's Jersey," I asked Maurice.

"Yes," he answered.

I admonished him to wear it when he came for the weekend. When the guys brought him to the house from the airport, you would have thought they had been old time friends. Later in the evening everyone put on their team football shirts. Maurice was inducted in the family as he proudly sported his Steeler shirt!

Maurice fit right in. We had good food, fellowship, family games, conversations and individual prayers spoken in a circle before dinner. The day blended in giving thanks to God. Black Friday's plans included a tour of Washington DC, the Martin Luther Memorial, and the Smithsonian Institute.

Saturday, Maurice and I went to the mall to shop for the grandchildren. He guided me into several jewelry stores, saying, "I would like to get an idea of what kind of ring you desire."

What was odd to me, Although, through casual conversation, Maurice had said, "if you marry me, you will not have to work." he had not specifically asked me to marry him, yet. So, for fun I agreed and tried on rings with diamonds bigger than my fingers, with attached price tags that would stretch across an ocean. Maurice never flinched! I was impressed by his reactions. My kind of man!

Afterwhile, however, I lost interest in the search.

*He has not asked you to marry him.* I kept reminding myself.

I kept that thought in mind as we approached the second floor of the mall and entered another jewelry store.

*Wow!*

He coached me to follow him into the store. I surveyed the bridal displays. I was not impressed at all, until I saw the one. There it was standing alone. It twinkled, glistened, and beckoned me to take a closer look. I asked to try it on. It fit and I loved it! It was two carats of heavenly bliss.

I turned and asked Maurice, "Can we take this one home?"

He said, "Yes, we can."

We were escorted to a booth where the ring was examined under a microscope and was given visual and verbal certification. Maurice removed himself to take care of the finances. As I sat waiting for his return, he stepped back into the booth, kneeled on one knee in front of me, recited a speech, and asked, "Will you marry me?"

Between crocodile tears and a squeaky voice, I answered, "YES."

He placed the ring on my finger with a warm embrace. The attendants in the store were clapping and crying while wishing us, "congratulations!"

Shoppers passing by joined the celebration.

Both of us were blissfully overwhelmed with emotions.

Before leaving the mall, we stopped at the food court to share a large size soft drink. Our visual embrace with each other was locked in wonderment. We were besieged in delightful emotions.

When we returned to the house, I raised my hand. I didn't have to say anything. The bling from the ring spoke, loudly.

The family was ecstatic! Some were texting, while others were on their cell phones verbally sharing the news. All were cooing over a wedding on the horizon. The original plans of the wedding would be held in Pittsburgh. The date of the wedding was scheduled for September fifth tenth, two thousand, thirteen.

We began preparations. Our children and grandchildren would be our wedding party.

# Chapter Thirty-Four: Standing on His Word

*Faith and Family*

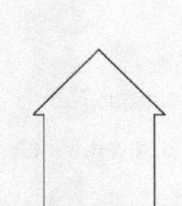

*When the consultation was over, Maurice said, "Because we are getting married, I wanted you to know what was happening with me. You can decide whether you want to proceed with the wedding."*

When I got back home, I shared the good news with my mother. She was beaming with joy. As the days and weeks passed, I shopped for the wedding. By the end of February, most of the plans were in place. Before March debuted, I received two phone calls from Maurice.

"Can you fly to Florida for the weekend?"

"Yes," I answered cautiously. "What's wrong?"

"I want you here with me for the follow-up consultation with the Urologist," he revealed. "I want you to hear the information firsthand."

Of course, I agreed. Maurice purchased round trip tickets and made a hotel reservation. Upon my arrival he checked me into the hotel, and we proceeded to the doctor's office.

"Mr. Jenkins, your test and biopsy reveals that you have prostate cancer." The Urologist said and went on to explain Maurice's prognosis and available options. This was the first time either one of us were hearing these details. His PSA results had risen from a four point six to an eight.

In previous year check-ups, there was no evidence of cancer. The progression went from four and a half to five, then six to seven. When the test revealed eight, his Urologist suggested because of the reading a biopsy was needed for further clarification.

Hearing this, I sat there numb and unresponsive.

*How could this be?* I asked the Lord silently. I was shaken to my core. I remembered the promise from the Lord and the confirmation, "He is the one-your husband."

When the consultation was over, Maurice said, "Because we are getting married, I wanted you to know what was happening with me. You can decide whether you want to proceed with the wedding."

I heard every word Maurice was saying, but I was heavily entrenched in thought. With a heavy heart, I responded.

"The Lord said that you are my husband," I reminded him. "And I stand on His Words by faith. We will go forward and get through this." I was fighting back tears, trying to appear strong.

Flying back home gave me opportunity to have quite time with the Lord. I felt so bad for Maurice. He was such a brave soldier. He accepted the doctors report with grace and dignity. I began to pray for his complete healing. I believe there is nothing that God can't solve.

He was a stellar man to include me with his sensitive, personal information.

As weeks moved closer to the wedding date, I received call number two.

"Are you sitting down?" Maurice asked.

Reluctantly, I answered, "Yes."

"My daughter and her family are not financially able to make the trip for the wedding."

My thoughts were moving in a thousand revolutions. I was searching for an answer. Finally, I had a suggestion.

"I could move the venue to Florida," I said tentatively.

After consultation with my family, the children and grandchildren were on board with the change. I also had a small delegation of family and friends who also committed to the change. My decision to change venues would give his children and grandchildren the opportunity to be included in the processional. However, I soon learned through rehearsal that his children did not accept me. My generosity was not reciprocated.

What should have been a glorious covenant celebration with the blending of families, had negative undertones.

Maurice and I had planned the roles of the wedding party: Michele, would serve as maid of honor and Michael, would escort me halfway down the aisle. Ron served as second escort and stood in for the father of the bride. Our grandsons served as ushers. Maurice's youngest granddaughter served as the flower girl. My youngest grandson served as ring bearer and escort for the flower girl. His daughters insisted their family stand on their father's side. This was awkward. My children represented the bride's side. It was uncomfortable, yet doable to keep peace.

The ceremony was beautiful.

I presented to him for a wedding gift a white chauffeur driven Royals Royce. We honeymooned in Hawaii, on the island of Maui for seven days.

# Chapter Thirty-Five: A Garment of Praise

In the Embers

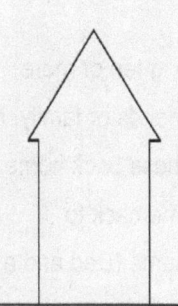

*We look back now with praises of thanksgiving for what the Lord has done, and where He has brought us-into a wealthy place. Our marriage has evolved to greater depths of compassion, heights of strength and widths of love. I am so grateful, even when the furnace of evil was turned up seven times hotter against us, I did not throw in the towel. Not only has the Lord blessed us, but we have also become a conduit of blessing to others.*

The next three and a half years were painful. A terrible, heart-wrenching lie was hailed against Maurice and I. As a result, his family and children in Florida turned against us. The poison had even seeped into the ears of some of our church congregants. Both of our witness for Christ along with our character were being assassinated.

We were being accused of infidelity before Maurice's wife transitioned. But remember, I lived in Pittsburgh (a thousand miles away)!

At first, we had no idea of the existence of the lie or its origin. However, it was only after the tremendous pain it caused us, that we discovered it was his brother-n-law and oldest daughter who were at the center of this controversy. Their claim was predicated on Maurice's former wife's mention of a *Marie* who prayed with her, spent time with her, and spoke with her on the phone. We discovered, the *Marie* she mentioned was her Naturalist, not me. (The Naturalist Practitioner was the person she turned to, as an alternative to conventional treatments and medications.)

When all of this was occurring, Maurice was still working ten or more hours a day. This left me alone without support from friends or family. I would not disclose the pain we were experiencing to those back home. I am confident my children would have come and took me back to Pittsburgh. Their love for Maurice was evident in the name (Dad and a special name Daddy-babe) given by Michele. One which she did not allow anyone else to use. (Now close friends call him Daddy-babe). Michele arrived at his special name by blending Daddy and Babe, which I call him.

Maurice was not the reason for the problems in our marriage, so leaving him would have been devastating. We made a vow to each other and to God, that only death would part us, and I was determined to honor it. So, I decided to stay and endure my pain in silence.

Living in an environment where you are consistently viewed through a false lens of condemnation manifested mental trauma to the point where I had trouble sleeping at night. My dreams continually interrupted my rest with torment. The same dream occurred consistently:

I was falling down a dark hole with my arms extended up-ward, crying out for help, yet not hearing a response. These dreams still haunted me, even after we discovered who communicated the lie.

But in stepped God, into the mist of our situation which seemed so dark and unhappy.

First, the Lord healed our pain. Then He gave us a garment of praise. Finally, He washed away the stench of reproach and replaced it with the sweet fragrance of truth. Importantly, He gave me the ability to forgive those who trespassed against us. **Matthew 6:9 KJV**

It is one thing to read this passage from the Lord's Prayer in the Bible, it is another to successful accomplish those words with victory. Even though we had to suffer. The Lord reversed the curse and made it for our good. We are living the testimony of our best life.

After Babe (my husband) retired, we have been able to start on our bucket list of destinations. My first experience on a cruise ship was the Royal Caribbean. Our statesman room had an outside patio. Each night while we dined, the waiters entertained us. The Caribbean trip included the Florida Keys, Jamacia, Cozumel islands and more. I was just intrigued by the entrepreneurship of the island residence. We booked excursions ranging from zip lining, rode all-terrain vehicles, and took a historical tour covering slavery. Finally, we went canoeing. (We would never win trophies due to our lack of boating skills.) We took a seven-day guided tour of Israel with the Saints from Western Pennsylvania,

First Jurisdiction. Israel brought many Bible locations to life. And if that wasn't enough, our youngest son provided us with a ten-day all-expense paid trip to Italy.

These were all trips of a lifetime. We have time to enjoy each other taking road trips, flying to see the kids, using our time share, going to several costal destinations in Florida, D.C., South Carolina, Naples, New Orleans, Louisiana, Savannah, Atlanta, Massanutten, just to mention a few.

We look back now with praises of thanksgiving for what the Lord has done, and where He has brought us-into a wealthy place. Our marriage has evolved to greater depths of compassion, heights of strength and widths of love. I am so grateful, even when the furnace of evil was turned up seven times hotter against us, I did not throw in the towel. Not only has the Lord blessed us, but we have also become a conduit of blessing to others.

My praise or prayer did not diminish when my husband, in the year 2020 had his right thyroid removed. He had a phenomenal team of doctors. He went in for surgery on a Thursday morning. You can't even see where he was cut. After being released that following Friday morning with a clean bill of health, we went and had breakfast.

In the same year, the day after Christmas, I contracted Covid-19. My husband did not get the disease and was able to take care of me. I did not have a hospital stay, didn't need oxygen or a respirator. I stayed home under my husband's watch and Doctor's care, who called each day. My husband took my temperature every couple of hours. He measured the oxygen content in my blood using an oximeter and recorded all findings on a spread sheet located on his phone. I never lost my appetite, smell, hearing or sight. However, other than having children, I had not suffered pain like I did with Covid-19. It was a beast! My body felt like someone had scraped my flesh from my body and threw me in embers. I had unbearable pain.

I have the testimony that God is a Healer, a present help in the time of trouble. Our children were very concerned about us, but we did well!

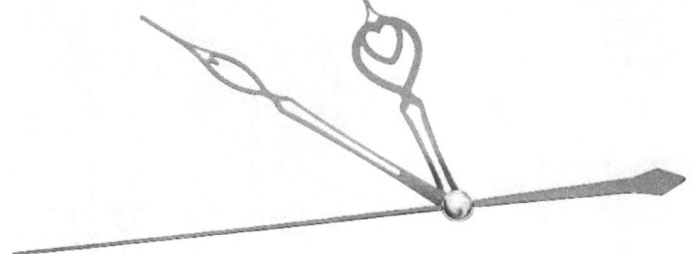

# Conclusion: Finally, Marie

*A Defined Space*

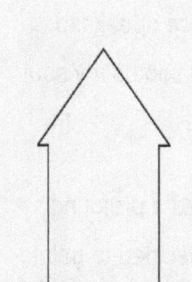

> God gave me the mantle to preach and teach His Word. The development of my vessel was molded in the crucible of my life's experiences. The higher degree of heat, the greater the change and development. I am so grateful for the encouragement, sacrifices, support, and love from my parents. But, most of all for the gift of Christ.

I have found my own space. I do not have to fit in with others. When I measure my present state of being against my yester years, I realize I have developed into the woman God created me to be. I no longer own depression, sadness, low self-esteem, or long for acceptance. I am no longer weighed by opinions, criticisms, or judgements from others.

Being present in the moment is an ongoing activity of self-examination. I am better today through the shedding of negativity. Mistakes are likened to a paradox (seemingly contradictory) to a positive outcome. Finding the message of positivity has led me to a secure, healthy, sound surrender. It is a place where one meets oneself for divine intervention. It is a place of truth, vulnerability, and acceptance. It is the space of do or die, face to face, relevance, revelation, absorption, and actuality.

Embracing realness is the dew that moistens the fiber of my being, preparing my heart and head for the adequate saturation of water needed to grow and glow within the glory and will of God. I fully embrace the gift that Jesus Christ left for us and gave to us, His peace. God's peace wraps me in His divine warmth. When situations in life are confusing, out of control, dark and disturbing, His peace speaks to those things dismantling storms, while His claims and sooths my soul. His manifestations are in His promises to the believer.

After about a year into the marriage with Maurice, I had a profound encounter with the Lord. My husband was at work. I decided to paint. While washing out the brushes and singing, I audibly heard the voice of the Lord speak. He said, "The sin you have preached and taught against, some are in you. If you want to be elevated in me, repent from gossip, backbiting, unforgiveness and anger. Do your first work over."

I was so out done!

I looked around to make sure no one else was in the same room. Conviction gripped my heart. Tears began to flow down my checks. My breathing became heavy.

*How could this be? Lord you know I love you.* I repeated over and over.

Through swollen eyes, I stood in transparency before a Holy God, surrendered and repented in obedience. The Lord reminded me what He spoke in, **Jeremiah 29:11**, "For I know the thoughts that I think toward you, saith the lord, thoughts of peace, and not of evil to give you an expected end." **KJV**

This is the first time in my life where my thoughts are free flowing and unhindered by its contents. I can remember events in my life as far back as my childhood. I ponder different situations, some pleasant and some not so pleasant. Yet, my emotions are not held captured to distasteful memories. My total being gives glory to God. Through my good, my bad and even ugly, He has never left me alone. When I came to the end of a bridge, He already had construction plans in progress extending the bridge to the other side for my safety. Looking back propels my thoughts for a brighter future. Now, I am grateful for past and present struggles. Past struggles were the conditions for my readiness in focusing on the call from the Creator of life. Present struggles, keeps me mindful of the passion, push, and press towards the mark of the high calling in Jesus Christ. My perfection in Him was developed through my trials. Now, I chase perfection, daily. God added value to my life. It has sustained me from yesterdays to be present in this moment to share *My Story*. I owe my life to Him.

God. I remember:

-the little girl with the marred body, ostracized from the class, placed in the corner, oozing boils of puss, criticized and lonely

-the 17-year-old daughter becoming a wife and mother who brought shame and disappointment to her Pentecostal parents

- feeling scorned, rejected, and bearing the Scarlet Letter over the divorce

-being stricken with grief from the death of a spouse and a single struggling mother, set-up for failure, and dishonor

-resurging with new life, new marriage, and more children

-widowhood, depression, disappointment, fear, grief, dwindling of dignity, loss of employment, crying for help, even the loss of life itself

My life is a tapestry of testimonies of how God's divine grace and mercy operates. I was broken into pieces with sharp edges, sometime flat, sometimes unrecognizable from its original design, with a variety of random patterns. But the Lord reshaped and formed me into a beautiful kaleidoscope of color and new purpose. I have been cold, hungry, lost, despised, forgotten, dismissed, overlooked, and neglected. I have been a succession of change. But the Lord never forgot about me and delivered me out of everyone. In this season, He has enlarged my tent. I embrace the quote David pinned:

"I have been young, and now am old; yet have I not seen the righteous forsaken, nor his seed begging bread." **Psalm 37:25, KJV**

The Lord is my Shepperd! He delivered me from a terrible pit, placed me in the palace. This is not just another story; it is a testimony! This is an account of how the Power of God can elevate you from any situation.

He can turn darkness, into light, pain into praise, wounds into worship, scars into salvation, singing blues into gospel songs of joy.

I am no longer in it; I am looking back on it! I am a survivor, delivered, victorious, walking in prosperity.

I thank the Lord for answering my prayers allowing me to raise my three children. Each one of them have and continue to be productive citizens - reinvesting in themselves, giving back to their community, and reaching out to help their fellow person. I have a great appreciation for Godly parents. They fulfilled the scripture,

"Train up a child in the way he should go; and when he is old, he will not depart from it." **Proverbs 22:6, KJV**

God gave me the mantle to preach and teach His Word. The development of my vessel was molded in the crucible of my life's experiences. The higher degree of heat, the greater the change and development. I am so grateful for the encouragement, sacrifices, support and love from my parents. But, most of all for the gift of Christ. I think of all the people I have been acquainted with throughout this journey of life. So many of them empowered me to be the best that I can be. Even the people who caused me pain, I have forgiven them and only wish them well. In this season of my live, it is comforting to watch the next generation of our family, the children, grandchildren and great grandchildren write their own story as part of our legacy. They are now cup bearers for justice and freedom fighters for peace.

*Marie Jenkins', My Time*

No more chains holding me:

There is a new chapter to *My Time*. There is an addendum to *My Story*.

Both have increased, expanded, and now include *Our Time!*

Maurette Brown-Clark's recording, "The One He Kept for Me" serenaded every step I took down the aisle, into the arms of …

> *"The one I waited for, my loves design.*
> *The one He kept for me, until it was time.*
> *The one I dreamed about.*
> *The one I can't live without.*
> *I prayed and waited for you so patently,*
> *and He's blessed our love for eternity.*
> *The one I was praying for,*
> *the one He delayed me for."*
> *…my babe, the love of my life, Maurice!*

I am living in the overflow of anticipated blessings. This season has been knitted by "a threefold cord is not quickly broken." **Ecclesiastes 4:12b, KJV**

The Father, Son, and Holy Spirit binds us together. We are locked in love with each other. Our hearts are devoted to God and the ministry He assigns. I am free of chains, restraints, obstacles, or inhibitions. I am free to be me, free to explore beyond boundaries, free to soar, free to dream, free to go forth, free to share heart thoughts, free to love and be loved. To be free releases dead bondage and captivity, the inner person, the agent within, struggles to be heard, to manifest with the expectation of acceptance.

We, (Maurice and I) overcame tremendous struggles. We held on to our commitment to each other and our faith in God. Today is a brighter day. I can see clearly; the sun is shining. He has added love, patience, support, laughter, and godly wisdom to my life.

Together, we have written additional chapters that belong exclusively to us.

## Photo Gallery
*Our Family*

*Photo 5 Our Daughter: Phenomenal, Ordained Minister, dedicated wife, compassionate, License Clinical Social Worker. Our Son-in-Love: Ordained Minister, Correction Facility Officer, Trained Chief*

*Photo 6 Our Son Extraordinaire-Musician, Music Producer, Entertainment Manager*

*Photos 7, 8, and 9: Grandchildren & Great grandchildren*

*Marie Jenkins', My Time*

Photo 10 After church following Michele's message

Photo 11 Maurice's youngest daughter & granddaughter

Photo 12 Our Son: Decorated Soldier, Vice-President, amazing Father, dedicated Husband. Daughter-in-Love: Military Service, great mom & wife

*Photo 13 Author and brother Joe: Rivals in childhood, defenders of each other in adulthood*

*Photo 14 Author and brother*

## Photo Gallery continued
*Our Wedding*

*Photo 15 "Our day Has Come."*

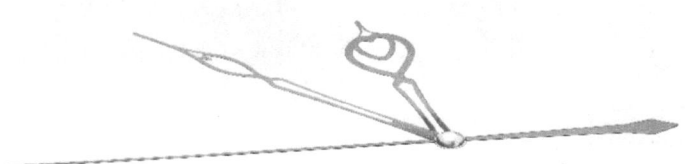

*Photos 16 & 17: Bride, Bride & daughter walking down hotel corridor*

Photo 18 Chauffer standing in front of Rolls Royce

Photo 19 "Elegance, beauty and love."

*Photo 20 "I am a blessed man!"*

*Photo 21 "Finally Marie!"*

## About the Author

Marie Annette Jenkins
*Evangelist and Author*

From the age of six years old, Marie Jenkins developed a passion for the Word of God. The seed was planted by her father, the late Pastor Samuel Williams. Her spiritual development increased through the years. Her maturity and anointing elevated her to the position of Evangelist, culminating in the appointment to District Missionary. In this appointment, Marie supervised the Women's Department of five Western Pennsylvania churches. She also served as a teacher and facilitator for the Minister & Missionary Alliance Institute and was a Board Member for the Church of God in Christ Licensure Committee.

Having served sixteen years in the Penn Hills School District and then working in the Mercy Behavioral/Mental Health system, the widow of thirteen years retired, relocated to Florida and pursued full-time ministry as a Licensed Evangelist.

In 2021, she authored her first book, My Time, which chronicles her life from early childhood through retirement. Acclaimed by the publisher as "...an inspirational body of work that is relatable to all and carries the reader through episodes of anguish, humor and grit."

Amid all her life events, Marie was sustained by her parental foundational teaching and faith in God. As a result, her ministry continues to expand beyond the walls of the church.

Married to Deacon Maurice Jenkins, she is also the mother of three grown children, six grandchildren and three great-grandchildren. The two are former members of the Macedonia Missionary Baptist Church congregation and are now currently attending West Orlando Christian Center, in Winter Park, Florida, under the tutelage of Superintendent Byron Stevenson, Pastor.

You may contact the author via email at: mariejenkinsauthor@gmail.com or via social media @AuthorMarieJenkins1

Additional Notable accomplishments:

- Carlow University graduate: Bachelor of Arts, Social Work, minor in Theology and Psychology
- National Honor Society member
- Facilitator & Keynote Speaker: seminars, workshops, revivals, retreats
- Single Adult Ministry and Couples Ministry Leader, Children's Choir pianist
- Advisor: Women's Intermediate Auxiliary, First South Florida Congress
- Deaconess Board, Facilitator

- District Congress of Christian Education, First South Florida Missionary Baptist Association
- Creator: *My Girls* (character-building initiative, girls ages 12-17)
- Creator: Zoom Family Bible Study Curriculum (during Covid-19 pandemic)
- Philanthropy: FLM HAITI, Educational & Medical Missions
- Educational and Musical Scholarship Programs: Bethune Cookman Choir
- Supporter: Shoes for African Children, The Kings Academy K-6
- Civic Contributions: Provided leadership and teaching Life Skills in a Summer Youth Program, Monumental Baptist Church. Creator of community service initiatives for the *Etiquette Dining Program*, ages 12-18, A Second Chance Inc. Supervised the *Bridge to Life* after-school program. Member-League of Woman Voters.

# O.U.R. T.I.M.E.

Photo 22 "wees married now!"

We owe unconditional reverence for we are

together infused in a moment of endearment

Our Story continues to be written and guided by God.

*"In everything give thanks:
for this is the will of God in Christ Jesus concerning you."*
1st. Thes.5:18 (KJV)

Photo 23 *"Leaving the old behind, starting a fresh future!"*

"We make good great!"

www.butterflytypeface.com

Little Rock Arkansas

www.ingramcontent.com/pod-product-compliance
Lightning Source LLC
Chambersburg PA
CBHW052103280426
43673CB00083B/430/J